Chain Mail Jewelry

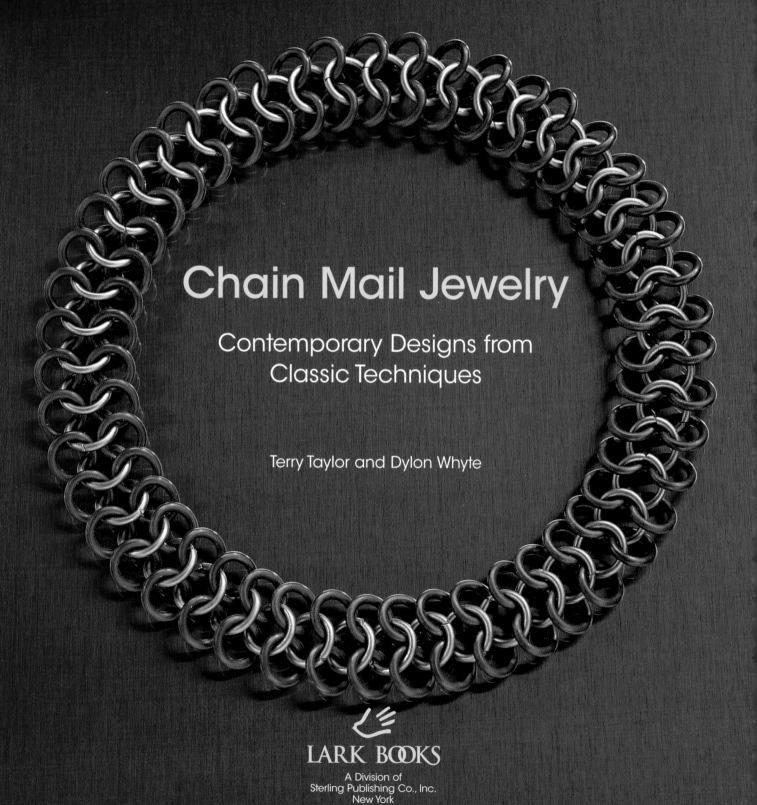

Chain Mail Jewelry

Contemporary Designs from Classic Techniques

Terry Taylor and Dylon Whyte

LARK BOOKS

A Division of
Sterling Publishing Co., Inc.
New York

EDITOR: Terry Taylor

TECHNICAL EDITOR: Dylon Whyte

ART DIRECTOR: Kristi Pfeffer

COVER DESIGNER: Barbara Zaretsky

ASSOCIATE EDITOR: Nathalie Mornu

ASSOCIATE ART DIRECTOR: Shannon Yokeley

ART PRODUCTION ASSISTANT: Jeff Hamilton

EDITORIAL ASSISTANCE: Delores Gosnell

EDITORIAL INTERN: David Squires

ART INTERN: Ardyce E. Alspach

ILLUSTRATORS: Dylon Whyte and Orrin Lundgren

PHOTOGRAPHER: Stewart O'Shields

Library of Congress Cataloging-in-Publication Data

Taylor, Terry, 1952-
  Chain mail jewelry : contemporary designs from classic techniques / [Terry Burgin Taylor, David Dylon Whyte].-- 1st ed.
    p. cm.
  Includes index.
  ISBN 1-57990-723-7 (hardcover)
  1. Jewelry making. 2. Metal-work. 3. Chains (Jewelry) I. Whyte, David Dylon, 1974- II. Title.
TT212.T39 2006
745.594'2--dc22

                                    2005030438

10 9 8 7 6 5 4 3 2

Published by Lark Books, A Division of
Sterling Publishing Co., Inc.
387 Park Avenue South, New York, N.Y. 10016

Text © 2006, Lark Books
Photography © 2006, Lark Books unless otherwise specified
Illustrations © 2006, Lark Books unless otherwise specified

Distributed in Canada by Sterling Publishing,
c/o Canadian Manda Group, 165 Dufferin Street
Toronto, Ontario, Canada M6K 3H6

Distributed in the United Kingdom by GMC Distribution Services,
Castle Place, 166 High Street, Lewes, East Sussex, England BN7 1XU

Distributed in Australia by Capricorn Link (Australia) Pty Ltd.,
P.O. Box 704, Windsor, NSW 2756 Australia

If you have questions or comments about this book, please contact:
Lark Books
67 Broadway
Asheville, NC 28801
(828) 253-0467

Manufactured in China

ISBN 13: 978-1-57990-723-5
ISBN 10: 1-57990-723-7

For information about custom editions, special sales, premium and corporate purchases, please contact Sterling Special Sales Department at 800-805-5489 or specialsales@sterlingpub.com.

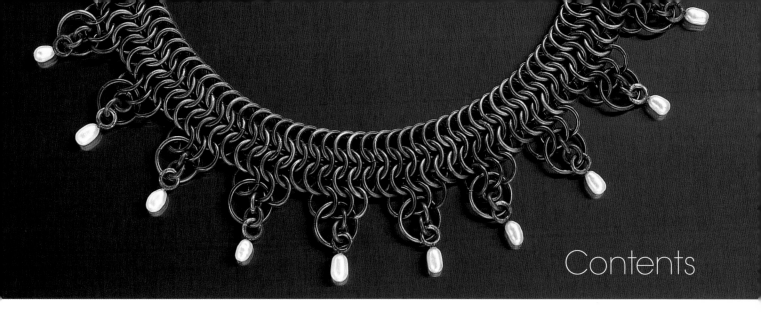

Contents

Introduction

Chain Mail. Do these words conjure up images of King Arthur's knights clad in *hauberks*? Do you envision ranks of Crusaders wearing *coifs* under their helmets as they march toward Jerusalem? Or, perhaps, you're picturing Renaissance fair re-enactors in hand-to-hand combat wearing *chausses*. All of these images of chain mail are accurate, but now take a look at a new way of seeing chain mail. This book presents 30 stunning chain mail projects for *adornment*.

Metalsmiths and jewelry makers have appropriated the construction techniques and patterns of the art of chain mail to create jewelry that is both a delight to look at and to wear. The weighty steel and iron rings that once made chain mail state-of-the-art protection have been elegantly supplanted by light-as-a-feather (and just as colorful) anodized aluminum rings, precious gold, sterling silver, and, yes, even those utilitarian neoprene O-rings of our modern mechanical age.

If you have two pairs of flat- or chain-nose pliers, you're almost ready to start. *Chain Mail Jewelry* gives you a handsome selection of projects that can be constructed using just pliers while you sit at your dining room table or even while you watch television. Thumb through the book and decide which project you want to make. Then, make a trip to your local bead store or go online to purchase jump rings for your project.

If you've never made chain mail jewelry, I suggest you turn off the television and pay close attention to the detailed illustrations. They're in this book for an important reason: they show you (better than telling you) exactly how each step of the project should look as you assemble it. Feel free to turn the television back on once you understand the basic principles of chain mail construction for the project you've chosen.

The projects in this book are organized by skill level. If you've never thought about making chain mail until now, start with a beginning level project. The Golden Lariat on page 45 is an excellent introduction to the classic 4-1 chain mail pattern. If a delicate lariat isn't what you're looking for, go for the bold Spiraling Chain on page 57. Want a contemporary look for your first piece? Then make one with neoprene rings like the Titanium Duet (page 20) or the Red and Black Cuff (page 60).

Perhaps you've tried your hand at simple chain making or even made a piece of chain mail before. If so, jump right in with an intermediate level project. A Japanese chain mail pattern such as the Lace Mail Cocktail Collar with Pearls (page 83) will intrigue you. Or try an advanced project like the Tasseled Snake Lariat (page 132).

Whatever your tastes, you're sure to find several projects you'll crave to make. Be sure to read the Basics section if you're a novice (it won't hurt to refresh your memory if you've dabbled with the craft beforehand, either). If you aren't interested in a copper piece of jewelry, there's no reason why you can't make the piece with sterling silver or colorfully anodized aluminum rings. If plain chain mail isn't your cup of tea, feel free to add beads, stones, or pearls to your piece.

Chain mail: it isn't just for protection anymore. Go ahead, adorn yourself with a single piece or create an entire jewelry box full of marvelous mail. *Chain Mail Jewelry* will show you how.

Chain Mail Basics

What Is Chain Mail?

No one knows precisely when or where the technique of interlinking metal rings to create a mesh structure—chain mail—came into being. Chain mail techniques have been used for centuries in both Japan and Europe. Archaeologists excavating 5th-century BC Scythian graves have found some of the earliest examples. We know that ancient Roman soldiers first came in contact with the technique when they invaded Gaul.

Bronze and iron links were typically used in early chain mail work. At first, individual links were hand-forged and riveted together for strength. From the 5th to 12th centuries AD, artisans perfected drawing thin metal strips through round holes in drawplates to form round wire. Coiling the round wire around a form became a quicker method of making the rings needed for chain mail.

Different linkage patterns for chain mail have been found in ancient sites around the world. European sites reveal use of a 4-1 linkage; Japanese examples favor a gridlike 4-2 linkage. Other linkage patterns were favored in the Middle East, specifically in Persia.

Chain mail garments—shirts (*hauberks*), hoods (*coifs*), and leg protection (*chausses*)—were used for limited protection to stop cutting weapons from piercing the skin in hand-to-hand combat. Through the 13th century, chain mail was common attire prior to the development of full suits of plate armor—those carapace-like suits for knights—which began to replace mail. However, mail was still used with plate armor, protecting the delicate and vulnerable parts of the body such as the groin and joints.

Chain mail fell out of fashion and was eclipsed by more modern technologies with the advent of modern warfare, but the technique lived on. Variations of chain mail fabric were used to create fine mesh bags carried by 19th-century ladies of fashion. Kitchen maids and housewives used pot scrubbers (the precursors of our abrasive pads) made of linked steel rings.

Chain mail is still in use today in several forms. Divers in shark-infested waters wear suits made of

Above: Mail shirt, 15th–16th century, western Europe
Collection of Higgins Armory Museum, Worcester, Massachusetts, USA

Left: Chain mail pot scrubber made of split rings

stainless-steel mesh that are impervious to shark bites, but not the bruises that will follow. Butchers and fishermen wear fine-mesh chain mail gloves to protect their hands from blades, saws, and hooks. Groups of enthusiasts re-create the arts and skills of pre-17th-century Europe in a variety of forms from tournaments of hand-to-hand combat to Renaissance fairs. These enthusiasts take great care and pride making authentic battle garb from literally thousands of steel rings.

Adapting chain mail patterns and techniques to create decorative, supple, innovative forms has gained wider audience in the last few years. More serious jewelers and bead enthusiasts have taken up this fascinating craft, using precious metals rather than steel or iron, to create wearable and fashionable jewelry.

Tools

Creating chain mail jewelry requires very few tools—far fewer than if you wished to set up a full-fledged jewelry studio. If you choose to work with purchased, commercially made rings, two pairs of pliers are just about all you will need. If you yearn to create your own rings, a few mandrels and cutting tools are essential. Torches and expensive polishing tools aren't necessary to make chain mail.

Pliers

Many different types and styles of pliers are made and each has its specific, recommended use. If you do beadwork or make other types of jewelry, you probably have the pliers you need to make chain mail jewelry.

You will need two pairs of pliers for opening and closing the rings to assemble chain mail. Pliers with flat faces—flat-nose and chain-nose—are best used with nonferrous metals such as copper, silver, and gold. They can also be used when working with aluminum and titanium rings. If you work with larger steel rings, more sturdy linesmen pliers are recommended.

Round-nose pliers aren't recommended for the opening and closing of rings, but they are certainly handy to have. If you're planning on adding beads

to your jewelry, you'll need a pair of round-nose pliers to create a wire loop (see page 15).

Every artisan has a tool with which he or she is most comfortable, whether it's a particular brush, a knife, or a potter's shaping tool. Pliers are *the* essential tools for making chain mail. You'll open and close *a lot* of rings—it's repetitive work—so comfort is important. Pliers with soft grips are highly recommended.

Purchasing pliers for chain mail work in a store rather than online or through mail order is an excellent way to find a pair you'll be comfortable working with. Pick them up; see how they feel in your hands. Examine the pliers' construction: for stability, a box joint is preferable to a simple overlapping joint. All jewelers develop a preference for tools they like to work with best. Some find that flat-nose pliers are best used with larger rings; chain-nose pliers with their smaller tips work well with smaller rings. It's a good idea to have two pairs of each on hand so you can work with rings of different sizes.

The pliers you choose to work with should have little to no serration on the jaws. The jaws should be smooth: serrations will mar the metal rings as you open and close them. You may find that the sharp, angled edges of the jaw will mar your rings as well, but this is handily taken care of by careful filing and sanding of the edges.

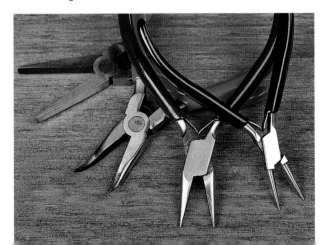

(L-R): Flat-nose, bent chain-nose, chain-nose, and round-nose pliers

Binocular headband magnifiers

Mandrels

Vision Aids

We can all use a little help with our vision, especially when doing work that demands detail. Even if your eyesight measures 20/20 in both eyes, lengthy, concentrated work sessions can strain your eyes and be extremely tiring. In addition, when you work with exceptionally small rings, it's more difficult to tell if a ring is completely and accurately closed.

A variety of tools can help to sharpen your vision while working. If you have little or no problem with your eyesight, the simplest vision aid is a pair of magnifying readers from the drugstore. Try on different strengths before purchasing a pair. Binocular headband magnifiers are very useful, even if you wear prescription lenses. They can be purchased in stores or online in different strengths, with and without focused lighting attachments.

Measuring Devices

A pair of calipers is a handy tool to measure wire thickness, the outer diameter of a ring, or the diameter of a mandrel. Having a pair isn't essential if you're purchasing your rings, but if you're winding them yourself it's an invaluable tool. Both digital and analog styles of calipers are available in most bead and jewelry supply stores.

A simple wire gauge is indispensable if—like me—you fail to mark coils of wire that you have stored away. The wire gauge pictured is made to measure nonferrous metal wire gauges from 1 to 36. On the reverse of the gauge are metric equivalents.

Mandrels

Winding your own rings to create chain mail jewelry is a worthwhile (if tedious) endeavor. If you choose to wind your own metal rings—rather than purchase them commercially—you'll need to stock up on a variety of metal rods in different diameters. It's acceptable to use wooden hardwood dowels to wind a few rings, but winding a considerable number of rings on dowels will not give you uniform sizing. Metal wound around a wooden mandrel tends to cut into the mandrel, decreasing the inner diameter of your rings.

It's quite simple to make your own mandrels with drill rod or steel tubing. Both of these materials are easily purchased from metal fabricators or hardware stores. Even metal knitting needles can be used as mandrels.

First, you'll need to determine the diameter of your mandrel. This dictates the inner diameter (i.d) of the rings you create. Use a caliper for the most precise measure of your

Digital calipers and wire gauge

mandrel. Once you have determined the size of your mandrel, you may wish to drill a hole in the rod to thread the end of the wire through. This makes it easier to tightly coil the wire around the mandrel. To remove the coil from the mandrel, you simply snip off the wire end you threaded.

If you become thoroughly obsessed with making chain mail jewelry (and you will), you may wish to look into more efficient and faster ways to make your own jump rings. A variety of manufacturers and suppliers have devised tools that wind long coils (longer than 12 inches) and provide stable, accurate cutting of the coils into individual rings.

Cutting Tools

Flush-cutting wire snips are indispensable tools for any sort of jewelry work. Other wire snips will work, but flush-cutting snips leave a less noticeable burr on the cut. This benefit is very important if you're winding and cutting your own rings. A noticeable burr will make the precise closing of the ring difficult and will scratch the skin if left on. If you are winding your own rings for use in chain mail jewelry, you'll want to invest in the best flush-cutting snips you can find.

A second option is to use an adjustable jeweler's saw frame and saw blades to cut metal coils into individual rings. This method is less likely to create a noticeable burr on the cut. It also leaves a thinner kerf (the gap between the ends of the ring after it is cut).

Below: Flush-cutting wire snips and jewelry saw
Right: Rock tumbler and ceramic medium

Polishing Tools

In general, little wear or scratching should occur as you assemble chain mail with either ferrous or nonferrous rings. However, sometimes polishing a piece is advisable to restore the bright finish that may have dulled from considerable handling while you worked.

It's impractical (and unsafe) to polish chain mail on standard rotary polishing wheels found in many jewelry studios. Similarly, it's not safe to attempt to polish chain mail with handheld rotary tools. Just don't do it.

Commercially prepared polishing cloths—the kind you find in jewelry and other retail stores—will be all you need to restore shine to a finished piece of chain mail jewelry. Look for those specifically designed to polish jewelry with microabrasives.

For tougher polishing jobs, many chain mail artisans use a rotary or vibratory tumbler. These simple tools—you may already know them as rock tumblers—can be filled with different types of polishing media: ceramic, plastic, or stainless steel. Each polishing medium creates a different type of finish. Many bead and jewelry supply stores stock inexpensive tumblers and a variety of media for use with them.

Tip: I use dry, *converted* rice as a tumbling medium to restore shine on copper and silver. It's reusable, safe, and cheap.

Dylon Whyte

Materials

The materials you'll need to create chain mail jewelry are not extensive. Most of the projects in this book were created with commercially prepared metal rings, neoprene rings, beads, and a few jewelry findings such as clasps and ear wires.

Wire

Any metal can be made into a wire form—silver, brass, bronze, gold, platinum, and more. In addition, some wires—primarily aluminum, copper, titanium, and niobium—are now readily available in a rainbow of anodized or dyed colors. Wire is made in a broad range of sizes (gauges) and shapes, or profiles, ranging from round to square, triangular to half-round.

Traditionally, chain mail is made from rings of round wire. Using round wire allows the chain mail mesh to remain flexible and supple. Different metals have different amounts of spring or strength. As you learn more and explore making chain mail jewelry, you'll develop a preference for the type of metal ring you work with.

The wire varieties used to create this book's projects are sterling silver, copper, aluminum, titanium, steel, and gold filled. It's a matter of preference whether you purchase commercially prepared rings and findings or use wire to create them yourself. Either way, you'll need to pay attention to the gauge of the wire specified in the project.

Wire gauge is a measurement that specifies the wire's diameter. On page 144 you will find a chart of wire gauges with the corresponding metric measurements for the two predominant systems of measurement used in the United States and UK. The larger the wire gauge number, the thinner the wire: 34-gauge wire is almost threadlike, while 2-gauge wire is almost a solid rod. Consult the chart when you are purchasing or winding your own rings.

Gold, copper, and silver wire are sold in four types of malleability: dead soft, soft, half-hard, and spring-hard. Wire stiffens a bit as you work with it. In fact, if worked too much, wire will become brittle and break. This is called work hardening. Purchase soft wire or half-hard to create your own rings: as you wrap the wire around a mandrel the process will harden the wire, but not enough for it to become brittle.

Winding Rings

If you choose to create your own rings, you'll need wire in the gauge specified in the instructions, a mandrel (page 10) to form the rings for the required inner diameter (i.d.), and a cutting tool (see page 11).

Left: Sterling, copper, and brass wire
Below: Wound wire coils

1 | Cut a length of wire and tightly wrap it around your chosen mandrel to form a coil. If you plan to cut the rings with a jeweler's saw, you should keep the coil relatively short, 1 to 1½ inches (2.5 to 3.8 cm). A short coil is easier to hold and saw.

2 | Slip the coil off the mandrel and tightly hold it in your fingers. Steady the holding hand on a bench pin or the edge of a table. Saw down the length of the coil, holding the saw at a slight angle. Be careful sawing rings apart—it's easy for the saw to slip and cut your fingers. With practice, you'll become adept at sawing coils.

3 | If you wish to use flush cutters to cut your rings, you can wind a longer coil. Slip the coil off the mandrel and slightly expand the coil. This will give you a small amount of room to position your cutters. Take care not to pull the coil too hard or you will distort the rings.

Commercially Prepared Rings

By and far the simplest way to make chain mail is to use commercially prepared rings—you eliminate the winding and cutting processes. The rings are uniform in size, cleanly cut, and, best of all, you can start constructing a piece of jewelry right away.

When you purchase rings you'll need to pay attention to three things: the inner diameter, the wire gauge, and whether the ring is cut or soldered closed. The i.d and wire gauge are important as they determine the look and suppleness of each piece of chain mail.

Each project in this book will specify both the i.d. and gauge of rings used. Most of the time you will be working with cut rings that you open and close. At times, however, you may want to use a closed ring for strength, especially when a clasp or finding is attached. When you purchase your rings, buy a few closed rings just for those purposes. If you forget to purchase closed rings and you don't have soldering equipment, most jewelry stores that offer repair will solder a few rings closed for a nominal fee.

Tip: It's wise to have some extra rings in each size needed for a project. You may mar some rings with your pliers or have a ring or two fly from the jaws of your pliers, never to be seen again.

Anne Kelly

A variety of sources offer both cut and closed (soldered) rings for making chain mail jewelry. Many local bead stores carry a somewhat limited selection of sterling silver and plated metal rings. Jewelry suppliers carry a wider selection of sterling silver and rings of other metals. Online suppliers offer an amazing array of rings specifically for chain mail in aluminum and steel, as well as precious and colored metals.

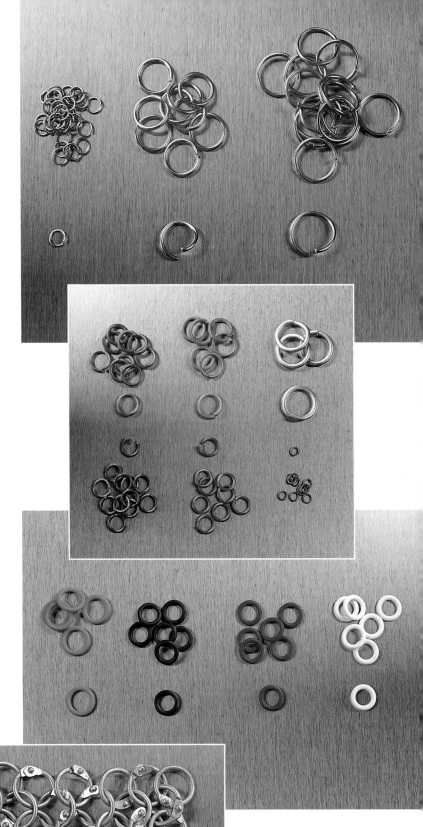

(Top to bottom): Sterling silver rings, anodized aluminum rings, neoprene rings, and riveted stainless steel rings

Jewelry Findings

Using prefabricated jewelry findings—if you don't possess the skills or inclination to make your own—is an excellent way to finish your chain mail jewelry. And it means you can wear your own creations right away, as well.

Necklaces and bracelets generally require clasps to keep them attached unless they are designed otherwise. Toggle clasps, lobster claw clasps, safety clasps, and spring ring clasps can all be purchased in a variety of metals to match your chain mail. Choose a clasp that complements the design of your piece.

Ear wires are generally made of metals—solid or plated—that are not irritating to sensitive earlobes. Bead and craft stores have many styles of ear wires to choose from. You can also purchase ball post earrings with soldered rings for pierced ears. These rings allow you to suspend chain mail directly from the ball post.

Head pins can be made out of any metal. These straight pieces of wire with a stopper—a flattened head like a nail, a ball, or a decorative fillip—are used primarily to attach beads to finished necklaces or bracelets. Head pins can be used to form simple earrings by adding a bead or two, then shaping the ear wire. You'll use head pins to attach beads and pearls to your chain mail jewelry.

Beads, semiprecious stones, and pearls

Beads

Knights of yore would *not* have attached beads to chain mail: they wouldn't have offered much protection. However, chain mail jewelry is another matter. Adding semiprecious beads, crystals, or pearls makes your chain mail even more elegant and adds a touch of color to personalize your piece.

The sky's the limit when it comes to adding beaded embellishments to chain mail. Semiprecious stone beads can be found in a wide variety of sizes, shapes, and cuts: round to pear shaped, smooth to faceted. Faceted crystal beads provide sparkle; sophisticated pearls can be purchased in a rainbow of colors, shapes, and sizes.

It's not difficult to add beads to your chain mail pieces, particularly if you have some experience with beading. You simply slip a bead onto a head pin and make a wrapped bead loop to attach it to a ring.

Above: A variety of clasps and bar ends
Right: Head pins

Making a Wrapped Bead Loop

1 | Slip a bead onto a head pin.

2 | Use chain-nose pliers to grasp the wire directly above the bead. Bend the wire at a right angle.

3 | Using round-nose pliers, position the jaws at the bend of the right angle. Wrap the wire over the top jaw of the round-nose pliers.

4 | Reposition the pliers with the lower jaw inside the loop. Wrap the wire around the pliers to finish the loop. Slip the loop onto a ring as directed.

5 | Grasp the loop with your chain-nose pliers and wrap the end wire around the wire stem to secure the loop. Trim off any excess wire.

Finishing Touches

Completed chain mail jewelry rarely needs serious polishing. Usually, a quick rub with a polishing cloth or a spin through a tumbler will make your chain mail jewelry sparkle (see page 11).

However, metal that is sparkling and shiny may not always be what you desire for your finished piece. You may prefer a matte finish or wish to change the appearance of your metal rings altogether. Through the ages metalsmiths have developed methods to change the surface appearance of metal through a variety of tricks—some created chemically and some through the application of heat.

The most common change made to most metals results from oxidation over time. In steel, this appears as rust; in silver, oxidation appears as a gradual dulling and darkening of surface and crevices. Copper will gradually darken or develop the green tones of verdigris. Bronze and brass also change color over time. Gold and some of the other precious metals such as niobium, palladium, and titanium-resist oxidation and retain their color.

Metals that will be affected by oxidation can be coated with lacquer or waxes to preserve their original finish. Lacquers, beeswax, paraffin, and commercial paste waxes are easily applied to chain mail to slow the darkening process. This should be done *before* attaching beads to a piece, as the wax may dull or alter the bead surface. Take care to avoid waxes that contain additives such as silicone that may be found in paste waxes for automobiles.

The simplest method of wax application uses a soft cloth. This process is made even easier if you warm the chain mail in a household oven at a low temperature. Make sure that the metal is just warm to the touch, then use a soft cloth to apply a thin coat of wax. This will slow—but not totally prevent—the process of oxidation, particularly on brass, copper, and steel. Reapplication of wax will be needed over time.

Patinas

Changing the surface appearance of metal may be accomplished through the use of chemicals, heat, or abrasives. Chemical changes are best used on metals after they have been assembled. Heat should be used to color metal before assembly. Abrasive treatments may be used at any time.

A simple patina solution to use on silver and copper is liver of sulfur (potassium sulfide). As it's name suggests, it is a somewhat unpleasant-

(L-R): Liver of sulfur on copper, brushed liver of sulfur patina, and untreated copper

smelling solution, but not unbearable. Liver of sulfur will create a spectrum of colors on silver, from gold to brown to red to blue to gray. It will darken copper but has no effect on brass or nickel silver. Check jewelry supply or bead shops for patina solutions created specifically for those metals.

Liver of Sulfur

Take care to avoid getting the solution on your skin or clothing. Using disposable latex gloves is an excellent way to prevent skin contact. Use a container specifically set aside to mix the solution in. Never use this container for food once it used to hold the solution. Work at a sink with running water.

1 | Wash the chain mail in a solution of warm water with a commercial scouring powder or grease-cutting liquid dish detergent. Dry it carefully.

2 | Dissolve a pea-sized piece of sulfur in a container of very warm water.

3 | Warm the chain mail piece under hot water. Dip the piece briefly into the solution, then quickly rinse it. Examine the color. Dip and rinse the piece until you have achieved a color you like.

4 | Buff the piece with a soft kitchen scrub pad (not steel wool) to selectively remove color from the metal. This will give your piece an antique look.

Matte Finish

Using tumbling media designed to produce a matte finish in a tumbler is an easy way to give your finished piece a nonglossy look (see page 11). A low tech solution is to buff your piece by hand with a soft, kitchen scrub pad (not steel wool) until you have achieved the desired matte finish. Keep in mind that matte finishes are more prone to oxidation; you may wish to protect this finish with a wax or sealant to slow the oxidation process.

Making Chain Mail

The building blocks of each and every chain mail pattern are the rings. *Lots* of rings. Learning to open and close rings with ease and care is one of the marks of good craftsmanship. A perfectly closed ring should have an almost imperceptible joint, feel smooth to the touch, and not grab the skin or clothing. Practice makes perfect, so take your time before starting a project: it will be worth the time and effort.

Use two pairs of pliers that you are comfortable working with and that are appropriate for the size of ring and metal you are working with (see page 9).

1 | Hold the cut portion of the ring in the 12 o'clock position between the two pairs of pliers, which are in the 3 o'clock and 9 o'clock positions.

2 | Use the pliers to twist the cut ends: one toward you and one away from you to open the ring.

3 | Move the ends back together (in the opposite direction from step 2). Push the ends toward each other slightly.

Tip: Never enlarge a ring by spreading the ends apart laterally. You'll wind up with a ring that is next to impossible to close properly.

Tip: Check your joints by holding them up to a light source. If you see light through the joint, it's not closed tightly enough. Run your finger over the joint: if your fingers can feel it, your skin will feel it.

Chain Mail Patterns and Directions

Once you've mastered opening and closing rings, making chain mail jewelry is simply a matter of using common linking patterns. Patterns have evolved over the centuries, and today's artisans are creating variations on centuries-old patterns. Variations in pattern terminology are common among chain mail artisans. Some refer to the European 4 in 1 or 4-1 as European 1 in 4 or 1-4, but the structure remains the same: four rings are connected to one ring. With this in mind, it should come as no surprise that a pattern such as Japanese 6 in 1 is made up of six rings connected to one ring.

In Japanese, the word *gusari* is used for mail. A second word—as in *hana gusari*—fully describes the pattern. Japanese patterns are composed of vertical and horizontal rings. Their appearance is different from European patterns because they are created with two sizes of rings, unlike their European counterparts. In addition, some Japanese mail patterns combine round rings linked with oval-shaped rings.

Pattern names such as Byzantine are also known as Idiot's Delight, Bird Cage, or Fool's Dilemma. As you work with different patterns, you'll learn to recognize the basic pattern structure no matter what the name.

Each project in this book lists the specific materials and suggested tools used to create the piece. Each designer specified the exact size and gauge of the rings used to create the finished project. The type of metal for rings is listed, but don't feel constrained by it. Feel free to substitute the metal of your choice. A different metal will not change the drape of the piece.

The drape or flexibility of a piece of chain mail jewelry is determined by the size of rings used. Serious chain mail enthusiasts frequently discuss aspect ratios—the ratio between the i.d. and the diameter of the wire. We won't discuss the mathematical intricacies of the topic in this book. All you really need to know is that aspect ratio affects both the appearance and flexibility of chain mail.

Using larger or smaller rings than specified will change the appearance and size of your finished piece. Larger rings will make it look lacier, smaller rings denser. Similarly, if you use a ring made of larger or smaller gauge wire than specified, it will also change the appearance of the chain mail. If you wish to precisely replicate a project, be sure to use the rings specified.

Once you become addicted to making chain mail jewelry, you'll want to create your own design by adapting patterns and construction techniques used in this book. That's the time to experiment with different wire gauges and ring sizes. For best results, create test samples with different sizes of rings made of inexpensive metals before you commit to sterling silver or other more expensive metals.

Each project has a photograph of the finished piece and, in some cases, detail shots that help you see precisely how the piece is to be constructed. Step-by-step written instructions and full-color illustrations are meant to be used in tandem: you will see precisely how a portion of the project should look at a specific step.

A systematic color code for the illustrations will be used throughout the project directions. As you work your way through the projects, the color code will become second nature to you and you won't need to refer back to this section as often. Until you can decipher the code, always refer back to this page to refresh your memory before starting each project.

- ⬤ Open jump rings that are being added, then closed, are red.
- ◯ Closed jump rings that red rings are being placed through are silver.
- ⬤ Closed jump rings and beads that tag along with open red rings as they are being attached are blue.
- ⬤ All other extraneous detail is black.

The most important detail to study when examining the illustrations is how red jump rings pass through silver jump rings before closing, as this is the key to how the various patterns are constructed.

European 4-1

The most common linking pattern—the one most people are familiar with—is based on a European 4-1 structure. That is, four closed rings are threaded onto one open ring. The open ring is closed and the unit is set aside. Additional units are created, and then joined together with a single open ring to create longer and wider sections of chain mail. Many of the projects in this book are based on this linking pattern.

European 4-1 Units or Chainlets

1 | Open 1 jump ring. Close 4 jump rings.

2 |

Place the open ring through the 4 closed rings. Close the open ring. This unit is most often referred to as a chainlet.

Assembling Chainlets

Once you have made *many, many* chainlets, it's time to assemble them into something that looks more like chain mail.

1 | Open 1 jump ring.

2 |

Place 2 chainlets end to end. Make sure that all rings are lying in the proper direction.

3 |

Place the open ring through the top 2 rings of the bottom chainlet and the bottom 2 rings of the top chainlet. Close the open ring.

Continue adding chainlets, repeating steps 1 through 3 to make your European 4-1 chain longer.

Be careful to check your chain to make sure that no chainlets have been added in an inverted manner as shown above.

Tip: Use a safety pin, twist tie, or even a plastic knitting stitch marker to mark the start of your work. Remember this tip especially when you are working the Byzantine pattern. You will also use a ring marker to remind yourself where you last left off in a pattern when you need to stop your work.

Dylon Whyte

Making the Chain Wider

1 | Open 1 jump ring.

2 |

Place a chainlet beside the European 4-1 chain. Make sure that all rings are lying in the proper direction.

3 |

Place the open ring through the 2 side rings from the new chainlet and 2 side rings from the existing European 4-1 chain. Close the open ring.
 Repeat steps 1 through 3 each time you start a new row.

4 | Open 3 jump rings.

5 |

Place a chainlet beside the European 4-1 chain so that it is above the chainlet added in step 3. Make sure that all rings are lying in the proper direction.

6 |

Place an open ring through the top 2 rings of the chainlet added in step 3 and the bottom 2 rings of the new chainlet. Close the open ring.

7 |

Place an open ring through the top side ring of the chainlet added in step 3, the bottom side ring of the new chainlet, and the 2 side rings from the existing European 4-1 chain. Close the open ring.

8 |

Place an open ring through the 2 side rings of the new chainlet and the 2 side rings of the existing European 4-1 chain. Close the open ring.
 Repeat steps 4 through 8 to continue each new row.

Titanium Duet

Designed by **Jerry Penner**

Classic black is subtly highlighted with periwinkle anodized jump rings. Use a bolder color—acid green or bright red—for a different look altogether.

YOU WILL NEED

122 anodized titanium jump rings,
    14 gauge (1.628 mm), 6.35 mm i.d.

194 rubber O-rings, 6.35 mm i.d.

Flat nose pliers

CHOKER

1 | Open 47 jump rings.

2 |

Place and close an open jump ring through 4 O-rings.

3 |

Place and close an open jump ring through 2 new O-rings and 2 O-rings from the previous step.
    Repeat this step 44 times, until you have a chain with 47 O-rings on each edge and 46 jump rings in the middle row.

4 | Wrap the choker around your neck to check the length. Add or subtract rings to the chain as needed.

5 |

Bring the 2 ends of the chain together. Place and close an open jump ring through the 2 edge O-rings from 1 end and the 2 edge O-rings from the other end to form a continuous choker, following the standard European 4-1 pattern.

21

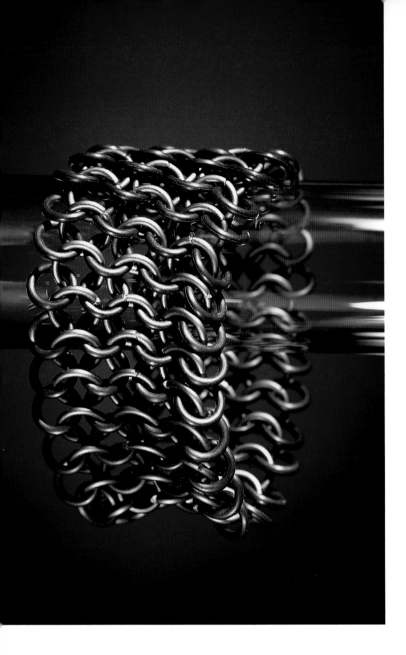

4 | Place and close an open jump ring through 2 new O-rings and 2 O-rings from the edge of the chain.

5 | Place and close an open jump ring through 1 new O-ring and 2 O-rings from the edge of the chain (1 of the edge rings and 1 of the new O-rings added in the previous step), as shown.
   Repeat this step 22 times, until you have added a complete row to the edge of the chain.

6 | Repeat steps 4 and 5 to add a 2nd complete row to either edge of the chain.

7 | Bring the 2 ends of the chain together. Place and close an open jump ring through the top 2 O-rings of 1 end and the top 2 O-rings of the other end.
   Place and close an open jump ring through the middle 2 sets of O-rings.

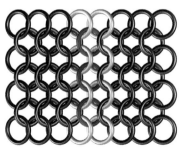

Place and close an open jump ring through the bottom 2 sets of O-rings.

BRACELET

1 | Open 75 jump rings.

2 | Follow steps 2 and 3 in the choker directions.

3 | Repeat step 4 in the choker directions 22 times, creating a chain with 25 O-rings on each edge and 24 jump rings in the middle row.

Hana-Gusari Anklet

Designed by **Rachel Dow**

This delicate piece of Japanese mail is made even lovelier with the addition of gemstone beads. Add extra length to the pattern to create a matching bracelet or neck piece.

YOU WILL NEED

50 large sterling silver jump rings,
   18 gauge (1.024 mm), 5 mm i.d. (A)

79 small sterling silver jump rings,
   18 gauge (1.024 mm), 3.5 mm i.d. (B)

7 gemstone beads, 4-7 mm

7 sterling silver head pins

1 sterling silver clasp

Chain-nose pliers

Round-nose pliers

Flush-cutting wire snips

1 | Close 43 large jump rings (A) and open 7 large jump rings (A). Open 79 small jump rings (B).

2 | Slip each bead on a head pin. Create a wrapped bead loop with each head pin as on page 15. Set them aside.

3 | Place and close an open large jump ring (A) through the loop of a head pin and bead combination. Repeat this process with all of the wrapped head pins. Set them aside.

4

Place and close an open small jump ring (B) through 2 closed large jump rings (A).

5

Place and close an open small jump ring through 1 of the closed large jump rings from the previous step and a new closed large jump ring.

6

Repeat step 5 until you have a chain that contains a total of 6 large jump rings. Place and close an open small jump ring through a large jump ring and head pin combination and one of the large jump rings from the end of the chain.

7

Fold the small chain back on itself to the left, so that the 5th large jump ring is below the 3rd and 4th large jump rings.

8

Place and close a small jump ring through the 5th and 3rd large jump rings.

9

Place and close a small jump ring through the 6th and 3rd large jump rings.

10

Place and close a small jump ring through the 6th and 2nd large jump rings.

11

Fold the chain back on itself to the right, so that the 7th large jump ring, which has a head pin and bead attached, is below the 5th and 6th large jump rings.

12

Place and close a small jump ring through the 7th and 5th large jump rings.

13 Repeat steps 2 through 11 to create a total of 7 triangles, each with an extra large jump ring attached.

14

Lay 2 triangles side by side, so that the 1st large jump ring (A) of the triangle on the right is beside the 4th large jump ring of the triangle on the left.

15

Place and close a small jump ring through the 1st large jump ring of the triangle on the right and the 4th large jump ring of the triangle on the left.

16 Repeat steps 14 and 15 to connect the 5 remaining triangles.

17

Place and close a small jump ring through the 4th large jump ring of the final triangle and a closed large jump ring.

18

Place and close a small jump ring through the large jump ring added in step 17 and the loop of the clasp.

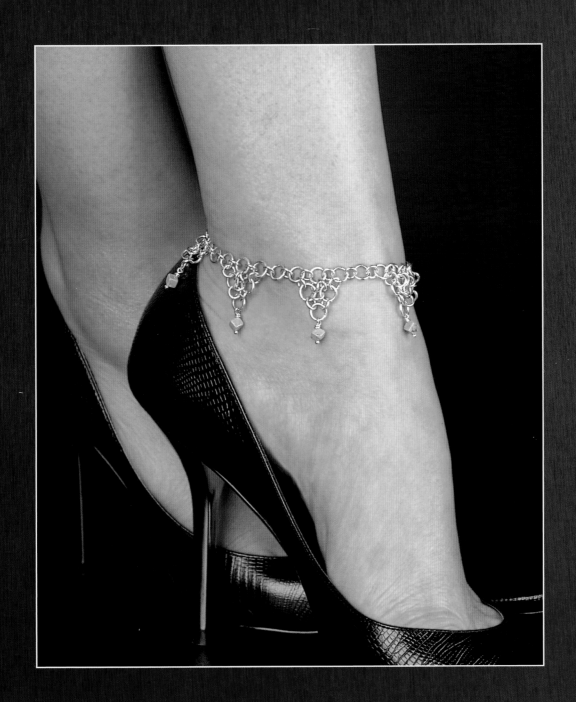

Japanese
Cascade Earrings
with Pearls

Designed by **Anne Kelly**

These earrings are elegance itself,
embodied in sterling and pearls.

YOU WILL NEED

36 large sterling silver jump rings,
   19 gauge (0.9119 mm), 3.97 mm i.d. (A)

128 small sterling silver jump rings,
   21 gauge (0.7239 mm), 2.38 mm i.d. (B)

8 fully drilled freshwater pearls, 5.5 mm

2 fully drilled freshwater pearls, 6.5 mm

10 sterling silver headpins

6 mm sterling silver post and ball earring findings

Chain-nose pliers

Round-nosed pliers

Flush-cutting wire snips

Note: For strength, the little ring on the post
and ball earring finding and the single ring
should be soldered shut. If you aren't
equipped to solder, a local jewelry repair
shop can solder them for a nominal fee.

1 Close 36 large jump rings (A) and open 126
   small jump rings (B).

2

Place 2 closed large jump rings together to
form a pair.

3

Place and close an open small jump ring (B)
through the pair of closed large jump rings
from step 2, and 2 new closed large jump rings
(A). Repeat, placing and closing a 2nd open
small jump ring through the same large closed
jump rings.

4

Repeat step 3 to add a 2nd pair of large closed
jump rings to the pair of large closed jump rings
from step 2.

5

Place and close an open small jump ring
through the closed large jump ring pairs added
in steps 3 and 4 to form a small triangle.
Repeat, placing and closing a 2nd open small
jump ring through the same closed large jump
ring pairs.

6

Place and close an open small jump ring through the closed large jump ring pair added in step 3 and 2 new closed large jump rings. Repeat, placing and closing a 2nd open small jump ring through the same closed large jump rings.

7

Repeat step 6 to add a 2nd pair of closed large jump rings to the pair of closed large jump rings added in step 3.

8

Place and close an open small jump ring through the 2 closed large jump ring pairs added in step 4 and step 7. Repeat, placing and closing a 2nd open small jump ring through the same closed large jump ring pairs.

9

Place and close an open small jump ring through the closed large jump ring pair added in step 4 and 2 new large closed jump rings. Repeat, placing and closing a 2nd open small jump ring through the same closed large jump rings.

10

Place and close an open small jump ring through the 2 closed large jump ring pairs added in steps 6 and 7. Repeat, placing and closing a 2nd open small jump ring through the same closed large jump ring pairs.

11

Place and close an open small jump ring through the 2 closed large jump ring pairs added in steps 7 and 9. Repeat, placing and closing a 2nd open small jump ring through the same closed large jump ring pairs.

12

Place and close an open small jump ring through the closed large jump ring pair added in step 6 and 2 new closed large jump rings. Repeat, placing and closing a 2nd open small jump ring through the same closed large jump rings.

13

Place and close an open small jump ring through the 2 closed large jump ring pairs added in steps 7 and 12. Repeat, placing and closing a 2nd open small jump ring through the same closed large jump ring pairs.

14

Place and close an open small jump ring through the closed large jump ring pair added in step 7 and 2 new large jump rings. Repeat, placing and closing a 2nd open small jump ring through the same closed large jump rings.

15

Place and close an open small jump ring through the 2 closed large jump ring pairs added in steps 9 and 14. Repeat, placing and closing a 2nd open small jump ring through the same closed large jump ring pairs.

16

Place and close an open small jump ring through the 2 closed large jump ring pairs added in steps 12 and 14. Repeat, placing and closing a 2nd open small jump ring through the same closed large jump ring pairs.

17

Place and close an open small jump ring through the closed large jump ring pair added in step 12 and 2 new large jump rings. Repeat, placing and closing a 2nd open small jump ring through the same closed large jump rings.

18

Place and close an open small jump ring through the 2 closed large jump ring pairs added in steps 14 and 17. Repeat, placing and closing a 2nd open small jump ring through the same closed large jump ring pairs.

Note: If you wish to stop here, you may skip to step 25, attach the findings, and you will have a nice pair of diamond-shaped earrings that the designer calls Five Row Japanese Earrings.

19 | Place all of the drilled freshwater pearls on head pins and create wrapped loops as on page 15.

20

Place and close an open small jump ring through the loop of a headpin and pearl combination. Repeat, placing and closing a 2nd open small jump ring through the loop of a head pin and pearl combination.

21

Place and close an open small jump ring through the 2 small jump rings added in step 20. Repeat, placing and closing a 2nd open small jump ring through the same small jump rings.

22

Place and close an open small jump ring through the 2 small jump rings added in step 21. Repeat, placing and closing a 2nd open small jump ring through the same small jump rings.

23

Place and close an open small jump ring through the 2 small jump rings added in step 22 and the closed large jump ring pair added in step 6. Repeat, placing and closing a 2nd open small jump ring through the same jump rings.

24

Repeat step 23 with the closed large jump ring pairs added in steps 9, 12, 14 and 17. When attaching to the closed large jump ring pair added in step 17, make sure you use one of the larger 6.5 mm head pin and pearl combinations.

25

Close the tiny ring on the belly of each ball and post earring finding. Place and close a single open small jump ring through the closed belly ring on the earring finding.

26

Place and close an open small jump ring through the small jump ring added to the finding in step 25 and the closed large jump ring pair at the top of the earring from step 1. Repeat, placing and closing a 2nd open small jump ring through the same jump rings.

27

Repeat steps 2 through 26 to create a 2nd earring.

Double Triangle Earrings

Designed by **Dylon Whyte**

Delightfully simple diamond shapes are given a graphic punch with the large silver rings. Add a small bead on the bottom tip or use a different color metal as the center ring for a bolder graphic look.

Basic Pattern: European 4-1

BEGINNER

YOU WILL NEED

2 large sterling silver jump rings,
    16 gauge (1.291 mm), 7.14 mm i.d. (A)

86 small sterling silver jump rings,
    21gauge (.724 mm), 2.38 mm i.d. (B)

2 ear posts with 4 mm drop loop balls

Chain-nose pliers

Ring marker (see page 18)

1 | Open 1 of the large jump links (A). Close 12 of the small jump rings (B).

2 |

Place and close the open large jump ring (A) through the 12 closed small jump rings (B).

3 | Open 30 small jump rings (B). You will be adding only small jump rings (B) in the next steps.

4 |

Separate 6 of the small jump rings that are attached to the large jump ring (A) and lay them so that they overlap, as in the standard European 4-1 pattern. Make sure that the overlapping rings are leaning to the left, as shown.

5

Place and close an open small jump ring through the 1st and 2nd small jump rings separated in step 4.

6

Repeat step 5 a total of 4 more times, placing and closing small jump rings through the 2nd and 3rd, 3rd and 4th, 4th and 5th , and 5th and 6th jump rings separated in step 4 to complete the 2nd row of the 1st triangle.

7

Place and close a total of 4 open small jump rings through the 1st and 2nd, 2nd and 3rd, 3rd and 4th, and 4th and 5th small jump rings added in step 6 to complete the 3rd row of the 1st triangle.

Place and close a total of 3 open small jump rings through the 1st and 2nd, 2nd and 3rd, and 3rd and 4th small jump rings added in step 7 to complete the 4th row of the 1st triangle.

9 Place and close a total of 2 open small jump rings through the 1st and 2nd and 2nd and 3rd small jump rings added in step 8 to complete the 5th row of the 1st triangle.

10 Place and close an open small jump ring through the 1st and 2nd small jump rings added in step 9 to complete the 1st small triangle. Place a ring marker on this small jump ring.

11 Repeat steps 4 through 10 with the 6 small jump rings remaining of the original 12 attached in step 2. When repeating step 4, make sure that the overlap matches the original step 4. When repeating step 10, do not place a ring marker on the small jump ring.

12 Place and close an open small jump ring through the single small closed jump ring at the tip of the marked triangle that was completed in steps 4 through 10 and through the drop loop of an earring finding.

13 For the second earring repeat steps 1 through 12. At step 12, instead of placing the open small jump ring through the single closed small jump ring at the tip of the marked triangle, place it through the single closed small jump ring at the tip of the unmarked triangle. (This will make the second earring a mirror image of the first).

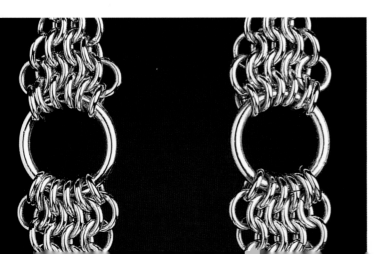

Gold and Amethyst Parure

Designed by **Emily Shore**

This delicate parure (set of matched jewelry) deserves special embellishments. Choose man-made crystals that satisfy your need for sparkle, semiprecious stones for luck, or pearls for their soothing sophistication.

YOU WILL NEED

459 gold-filled jump rings,
   20 gauge (0.8128 mm), 5 mm i.d.

43 size 8 (3 mm diameter) donut-shaped glass beads*

1 hook closure or lobster claw clasp

1 pair ear wires

Chain-nose pliers

* Make sure that the beads you choose slip easily onto the rings.

NECKLACE

1 | Close 196 jump rings and open 215 jump rings.

2 |

Place and close an open ring through 4 closed rings.

3 |

Place and close an open ring through 2 new closed rings and 2 closed rings from the base chain, following the standard European 4-1 pattern, as shown.

4 | Repeat step 3 until the base chain measures approximately 16 inches (41cm) in length and has 97 center rings and 98 edge rings. Lay the finished chain horizontally on your work surface.

Note: There are 3 different sizes of triangle drops: single (single ring and bead), double (2 rows made with a total of 3 rings and a bead), and triple (3 rows made with a total of 5 rings and a bead). The triangle drops follow a pattern of single, double, triple, and double, repeated 8 times and ending with a single triangle drop.

5 |

Place a bead on an open ring, then place and close the open ring through the first 2 bottom rings of the base chain. This completes the single triangle drop.

6 |

Place and close an open ring through the next 2 bottom rings of the base chain.

7

Place and close an open ring through the last bottom ring from step 6 and the next bottom ring of the base chain.

8

Place a bead on an open ring, then place and close the open ring through the 2 links added in steps 6 and 7. This completes the double triangle drop.

9

Place and close an open ring through the next 2 bottom rings of the base chain.

10

Place and close an open ring through the last bottom ring from step 9 and the next bottom ring of the base chain.

11

Place and close an open ring through the last bottom ring from step 10 and the next bottom ring of the base chain.

12

Start the 2nd row of the triple triangle drop by placing and closing an open ring through the rings added in steps 9 and 10.

13

Complete the 2nd row of the triple triangle drop by placing and closing an open ring through the rings added in steps 10 and 11.

14

Place a bead on an open ring, then place and close the open ring through the 2 links added in steps 12 and 13. This completes the triple triangle drop.

15 Continue the pattern across the necklace.

16

To finish, arrange the base chain vertically on your work surface. Place and close an open ring through the 2 end rings of the chain. Place and close a 2nd ring through the same end ring.

17 Repeat step 16 for the opposite end of the base chain.

18

Place an open ring through the hook closure or clasp, then place and close the open ring through the 2 rings added to the base chain in step 16. Place and close a 2nd ring through the hook closure or clasp and the 2 end rings.

19 Place and close 2 rings through the 2 rings added in step 17. Repeat until you have created an adjustment chain that is a total of 7 ring pairs in length.

20

Place a bead on an open ring, then place and close the open ring through the 2 links added at the end of step 19.

EARRINGS

1 Close 6 jump rings and open 18 jump rings.

2

Place a bead on an open ring, then place and close the open ring through 2 closed links.

3

Place 2 closed rings on a new open ring, then, holding the rings from step 2 by the bead, place and close the open ring through the 2 hanging closed rings.

4

Repeat step 3, placing and closing the open ring through the 2 hanging closed rings that were added in step 3.

5

Lay the earring flat, with the rows lying in classic European 4-1 fashion. Place a bead on an open ring, then place and close the open ring and close through 2 edge rings as shown.

6

Place a bead on an open ring, then place and close the open ring through the 2 closed links as shown.

7

Place and close an open ring through the ring added in step 5.

8

Place and close an open ring through the ring added in step 6.

9

Place a bead on an open ring, then place and close the open ring through the ring added in step 7.

10

Place and close an open ring through the 3 rings as shown.

11

Place and close an open ring through the 3 rings shown.

12

Place a bead on an open ring, then place and close the open ring through the ring added in step 8.

13 Place and close an open ring through the 2 rings added in steps 9 and 10.

14

Place and close an open ring through the 2 rings added in steps 11 and 12.

15 Place and close an open ring through the top 2 rings, including the ring added in step 13.

16 Place and close an open ring through the next 2 rings.

17

Place and close an open ring through the next 2 rings, including the ring added in step 14.

18

Place and close 2 open rings through the 3 rings added in steps 15, 16, and 17 and the loop of an ear wire to complete the first earring.

19 Repeat steps 1 through 18 to create a matching earring. If you wish to create a mirror image for the second earring, lay out the rings in step 4 in the opposite direction of the first earring.

King's Mail Bracelet

Bold (and beautiful) are words that accurately
describe this bracelet—for a man or woman.

YOU WILL NEED

- 128 large nickel silver jump rings, 16 gauge
  (1.291mm), 9mm i.d. (A)

- 12 medium nickel silver jump rings, 16 gauge
  (1.291mm), 6mm i.d. (B)

- 2 small nickel silver jump rings, 16 gauge (1.291mm),
  3mm i.d. (C)

- Clasp and toggle set

- Flat-nose pliers

- Needle-nose pliers

1 | Close 84 large jump rings (A) and open 44
large jump rings (A). Open 12 medium jump
rings (B).

 **Note:** Large jump rings are used to create the
bracelet itself. Steps 2 through 7 are worked
with large rings (A).

2 Place and close an open jump ring through 8
closed jump rings.

3
Place and close an open jump ring through the
same 8 closed jump rings in step 2.

4
Place and close an open jump ring through
4 new closed jump rings and 4 closed jump
rings from steps 2 and 3.

5
Place and close an open jump ring through the
same 8 closed jump rings in step 4.

6 | Repeat steps 4 and 5 nineteen times, until you
have a chain that has 20 internal ring pairs and
is 21 edge ring pairs in length.

7 Place and close an open jump ring through 4 closed jump rings from the end of the chain. Repeat, placing and closing an open jump ring through the same 4 closed jump rings.
   Repeat this step at the opposite end of the chain.

8 Place and close an open medium jump ring (B) through the 2 large jump rings (A) added in step 7. Repeat twice, placing and closing, in turn, 2 open medium jump rings through the same 2 large jump rings.

9 Place and close an open medium jump ring (B) through the 3 medium jump rings (B) added in step 8.

10 Place and close an open small jump ring (C) through the medium jump ring added in step 9.

11 Place and close an open small jump ring through the small jump ring added in step 10 and the bar half of the toggle clasp.

12 Place and close an open medium jump ring (B) through the 2 large jump rings (A) added in step 7 and the loop half of the toggle clasp. Repeat twice, placing and closing, in turn, 2 open medium jump rings through the same 2 large jump rings and the loop half of the toggle clasp.

13 Place and close an open medium jump ring (B) vertical through the 2 pairs of large jump rings (A) at the end of the bracelet as shown.

14 Repeat step 13 through the 2 pairs of large jump rings (A) at the same end, but opposite side of the bracelet.

15 Repeat steps 13 and 14 for the other end of the bracelet.

16 If desired, oxidize the completed bracelet with a patina solution.

Golden Lariat

Designed by **Rachel Dow**

A lariat necklace showcases the supple drape that you can achieve with chain mail. The simple addition of freshwater pearls makes this necklace a must-have for your jewelry collection.

YOU WILL NEED

420 gold-filled jump rings, 20 gauge
(0.8128 mm), 5 mm i.d.

4 freshwater pearls, 9-10 mm

4 gold-filled head pins, 22 gauge

Chain-nose pliers

Round-nose pliers

Flush-cutting wire snips

1 | Assemble 68 chainlets (page 18).

2 | Connect 60 of the chainlets to create a chain
approximately 32 inches (81 cm) in length
(page 18).

3 |

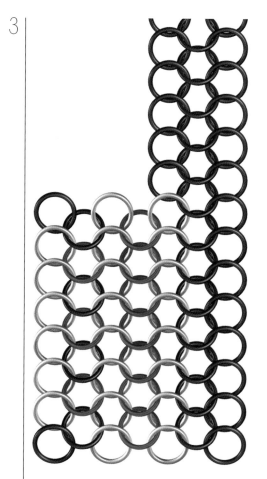

Attach 4 of the remaining chainlets to one end
of the chain, as shown.

4 |

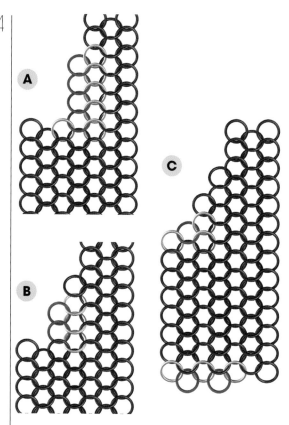

Taper the end of the chain by adding rings as
shown in A, B, and C.

5 | Place a freshwater pearl on each head pin.
Make a wrapped bead loop on the head pin
(page 15).

Add the freshwater pearls to the tapered
lariat end. Open the outermost corner ring,
place the head pin loop on the ring and close
it again. Add an open ring with head pin and
pearl to one of the end rings added in step 4.

Repeat steps 3 through 5 to finish the
opposite end of the chain, making sure to add
the 4-1 units in step 3 to the same outside edge
of the chain.

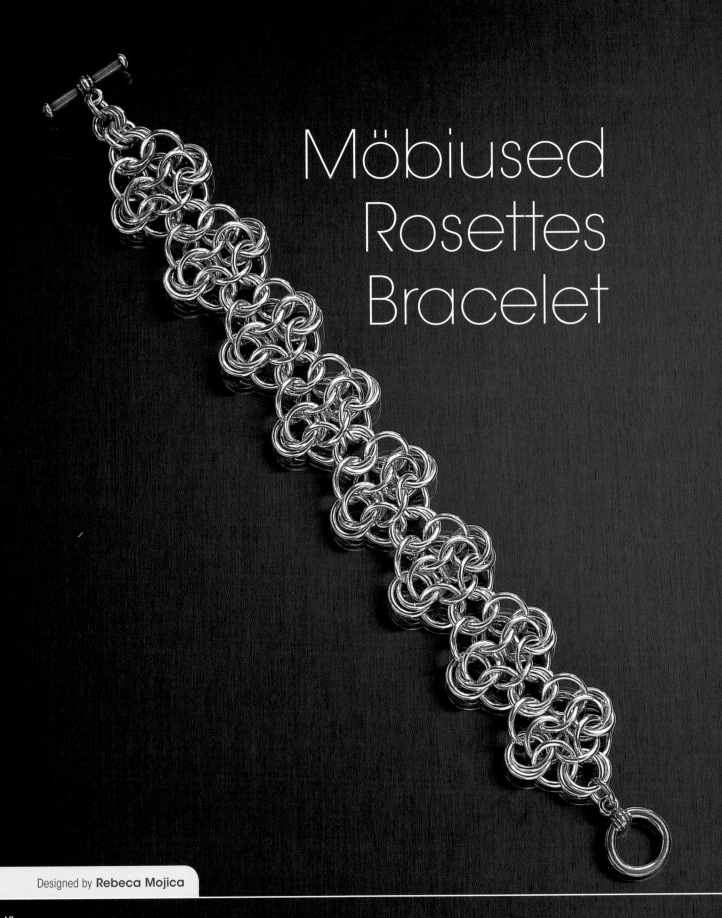

Möbiused Rosettes Bracelet

Designed by **Rebeca Mojica**

This variation of European 4-1 chain mail is given a "special twist."

It's the perfect project to make as a not-soon-to-be-forgotten gift.

YOU WILL NEED

114 large copper jump rings, 18 gauge (1.024 mm), 6.35 mm i.d. (A)

4 small copper jump rings, 18 gauge (1.024 mm), 3.97 mm i.d. (B)

1 copper-finish toggle

Flat-nose pliers

1 | Open 66 large jump rings (A), close 48 large jump rings (A), and open the 4 small jump rings (B).

Note: The body of the bracelet is created with large jump rings (A).

2 |

Place and close an open large jump ring through 4 closed jump rings.

3 |

Place and close an open jump ring through 2 new closed jump rings and 2 closed jump rings from the previous step, following the standard European 4-1 pattern.

4 |

Place and close an open jump ring through 2 new closed jump rings and the 2 closed jump rings from the previous step, following the standard European 4-1 pattern.

5 |

Place and close an open jump ring through the 4 closed rings from step 4 *and* the formerly open jump ring added in step 4, as shown.

6 |

Place and close an open jump ring through 2 new closed jump rings and the 2 closed jump rings from step 4, following the standard European 4-1 pattern.

7 | Repeat steps 3 through 6 six times.

8 | Repeat steps 3 and 4 once more. This creates a chain with a total of 8 groups, each with 3 edge links.

9

Place and close an open jump ring through the 2 jump rings at one end of the chain.

10

Place and close an open jump ring through the 2 jumps rings at one end of the chain added to in step 9 *and* the formerly open jump ring added in step 9, as shown.

11 | Repeat steps 9 and 10 on the opposite end of the chain.

12

Place and close an open jump ring through the 1st group of 3 edge jump rings on one end of the chain.

13

Place and close an open jump ring through the 1st group of 3 edge jump rings on one end of the chain added to in step 12 *and* the formerly open jump ring added in step 12, as shown.

14

Repeat steps 12 and 13 with the 1st group on the opposite edge of the bracelet.

15 | Repeat steps 12 through 14 for the remaining 14 groups of 3 edge jump rings on both sides of the bracelet.

16

Place and close a small open jump ring (B) through the 2 jump rings added in steps 9 and 10 and the loop of the toggle clasp. (Adding a 2nd ring will strengthen the connection).
  Repeat at the opposite end with the toggle bar.

Note: You may need to add a small length of additional doubled jump rings (B) so the bar has enough slack to be easily pulled through the loop.

Natasha Necklace

Designed by **Spider**

This necklace—a delicate wisp of a thing—commands attention with its sparkling touches of color.

B E G I N N E R

YOU WILL NEED

- 11 large sterling silver jump rings, 15 gauge (1.45 mm), 7 mm i.d. (C)
- 44 small sterling silver jump rings, 20 gauge (0.8128 mm), 3 mm i.d. (A)
- 141 medium sterling silver jump rings, 19 gauge (0.9119mm), 4.5mm i.d. (B)
- 11 beads
- 11 head pins
- 1 lobster claw clasp
- Chain-nose pliers
- Round-nose pliers
- Flush cutting wire snips

1 Open the 11 large rings (C) and close the 44 small rings (A).

Place and close one large ring (C) through 4 small closed rings (A). You will need 11 of these units for a 14-inch (36 cm) necklace. Set the units aside.

2 Open 141 medium rings (B). Connect the 11 units from step 1 with simple chains created with 7 medium rings.

3 Hold the first medium ring of the first connecting chain steady in your left hand, then grasp the last medium ring of the same chain in your right hand. Turn the chain toward you with your right hand until the rings twist and overlap, creating two rows of basic European 4-1 pattern chain mail.

4 Lock the new row of overlapped rings in place by placing and closing 3 new medium rings: 1 through the first 2 links, 1 through the 2nd and 3rd links, and 1 through the 3rd and 4th links. This creates a new row of European 4-1 chain mail.

Repeat steps 3 and 4 with the 9 remaining connector chains.

5

Add another row to the 4-1 sections by placing and closing 2 medium rings through the first 2 and 2nd and 3rd rings of the row created in step 4.

Repeat this step for the 9 remaining chain mail sections.

6

Before closing this medium ring, place it through the loop of a head pin and bead combination.

7

Attach the lobster clasp with a medium ring to one end of the necklace and add an adjustment chain of 10 medium rings ending with a head pin and bead to the other end of the necklace.

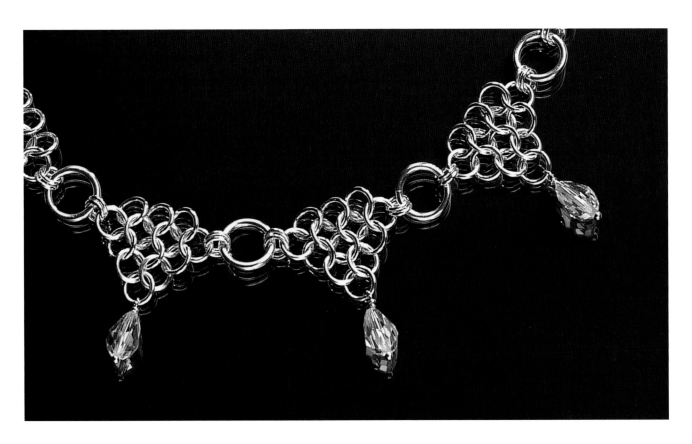

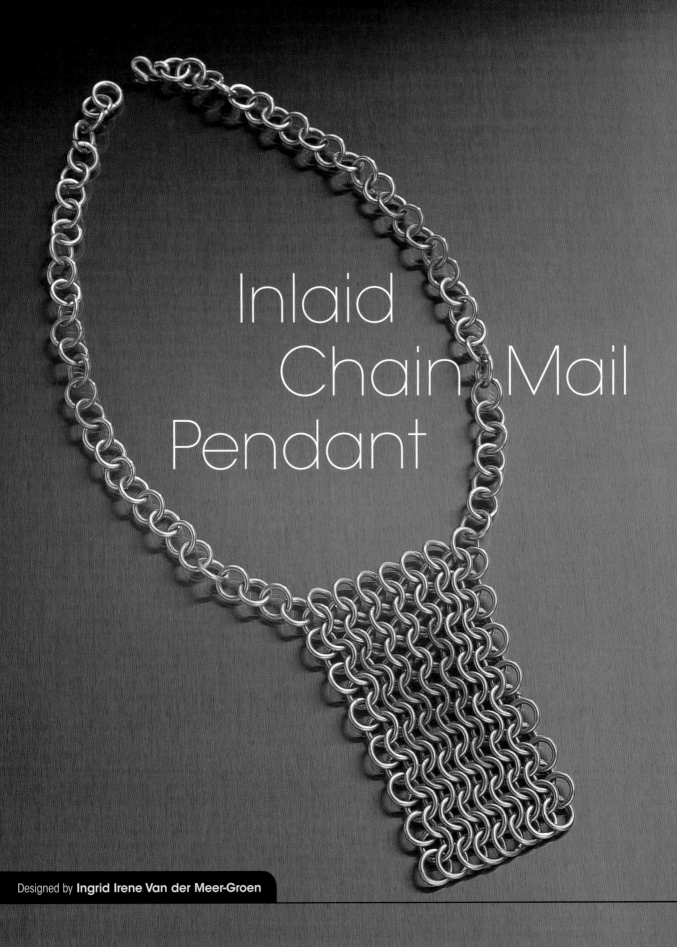

Inlaid Chain Mail Pendant

Pendant

Designed by **Ingrid Irene Van der Meer-Groen**

Once you've mastered constructing this pattern, try designing your own patterned pendant—your initial, a geometric shape? Use a sheet of graph paper to chart out your design, choose your colors, and then create your pattern.

YOU WILL NEED

160 anodized aluminum jump rings (bronze color), 14 gauge (1.628 mm) 6 mm i.d.

39 anodized aluminum jump rings (blue), 14 gauge (1.628 mm), 6 mm i.d.

Flat-nose pliers*

Round-nose pliers

* To avoid marring the delicate colored surfaces of the anodized rings, make sure the flat surfaces of your pliers are smooth (page 9).

Note: The illustrations in this project use bronze and blue to indicate where bronze and blue rings are added.

Review the instructions on European 4-1 on page 18.

1 | Open 159 bronze jump rings and the 39 blue jump rings.

2 |

Create 4 rows of European 4-1 mail from bronze jump rings. Each row should be 8 jump rings wide. The 4 rows are offset, alternating left and right.

3 |

Adding to the top of row 4, add 2 bronze jump rings, 1 blue jump ring, 2 bronze jump rings, 1 blue jump ring, and 2 bronze jump rings, right offset, to complete row 5.

4 |

Adding to the top of row 5, add 3 bronze jump rings, 1 blue jump ring, 1 bronze jump ring, 1 blue jump ring, and 3 bronze jump rings, left offset, to complete row 6.

5 |

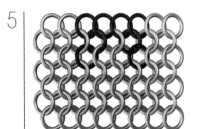

Adding to the top of row 6, add 2 bronze jump rings, 4 blue jump rings, and 2 bronze jump rings, right offset, to complete row 7.

6

Adding to the top of row 7, add 3 bronze jump rings, 3 blue jump rings, and 2 bronze jump rings, left offset, to complete row 8.

7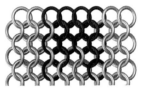

Adding to the top of row 8, add 2 bronze jump rings, 4 blue jump rings, and 2 bronze jump rings, right offset, to complete row 9.

8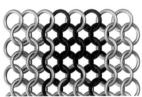

Adding to the top of row 9, add 3 bronze jump rings, 1 blue jump ring, 1 bronze jump ring, 1 blue jump ring, and 3 bronze jump rings, left offset, to complete row 10.

9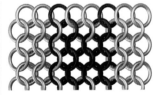

Adding to the top of row 10, add 2 bronze jump rings, 1 blue jump ring, 2 bronze jump rings, 1 blue jump ring, and 2 bronze jump rings, right offset, to complete row 11.

10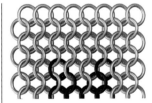

Add 4 more rows of bronze jump rings, with 8 jump rings per row, alternating with a left offset for row 12, right offset for row 13, left offset for row 14 and right offset for row 15 to complete the inlaid pendant.

11

Starting at the top left corner of the pendant, create a simple chain of 12 bronze jump rings, 5 blue jump rings, and 12 bronze jump rings.
   Make a 2nd chain starting at the top right corner of the pendant.

12 Create a clasp with a bronze jump ring. Twist the ring to form an S shape. Use round-nose pliers to make one half of the link closed tight and the other side just tight enough to slip over a bronze jump ring.

13 Place and close an open bronze jump ring through the final bronze jump ring of the left chain and the closed section of the hook.

14 Place and close an open bronze jump ring through the final bronze jump ring of the right chain, so that the hook is spaced evenly at the back of the neck.

Spiraling Chain

Designed by **Dylon Whyte**

This handsome chain will draw envied glances from one and all. Accept the glances with a graciously sly grin—only you will know how deceptively simple this chain is to create.

Basic Pattern: **Spiral 6-1**

BEGINNER

YOU WILL NEED

160 stainless steel jump rings, 16 gauge (1.291mm), 12.13mm ($7/16$inch) i.d.*

Ring marker (page 18)

Flat-nose pliers

* The number of rings represented here is for a chain that is 24 inches long; you can reduce or increase the number of rings to shorten or lengthen the chain.

Working Hint: The first 10 or 12 rings are always a little tricky to get started. You can re-twist the pattern if you drop the chain.

1 | Close 1 ring. Open the remaining 159 rings.

2 |
Place an open ring through the closed ring. Close the open ring. Place a ring marker on the 1st link.

3 |
Twist the pair of rings from step 2 clockwise. Hold the right-hand ring so that it is pressed against the top of the left-hand ring. Place 1 open ring through both previously closed rings so that it follows the same clockwise twist. Close the open ring.

4 |
Hold the rings twisted and place 1 open ring through the 3 previously closed rings so that it follows the same clockwise twist. Close the open ring.

5 |
Keeping the pattern twisted, place 1 open ring through the 3 previously closed rings so that it follows the same clockwise twist. This means that the original closed ring from step 1 does not have a new ring pass through it. Close the open ring.

6 | Keep adding rings as you did in step 5—each new ring passes through the 3 previous rings—following the same clockwise twist, until you have only 3 open rings remaining or the chain is the desired length.

7 | Twist clockwise and bring the 2 ends of the chain together. It is important to twist the pattern as you bring the ends together in order to keep the pattern tight. However, you do not want to over or under twist the pattern. Overtwisting will cause knots; undertwisting will untwist the pattern.

Following the clockwise twist, place an open ring through the 3 end rings of the left end of the chain and through the 1st end ring of the right end of the chain. Close this ring.

Following the clockwise twist, place an open ring through the 2 end rings of the left end of the chain, the ring you added in step 8, and the 2 end links of the right end of the chain. Close this ring.

Following the clockwise twist, place an open ring through the final end ring of the left end of the chain, the ring you added in step 8, the ring you added in step 9 and the 3 end rings of the right end of the chain. Close this ring.

Working Hint: I find that the best way to judge the right amount of twist is to twist the chain until it is stiff, before knots begin to form, then untwist (loosen) by two revolutions before attaching the ends.

Dylon Whyte

Red and
Black Cuff

Designed by **Cheryl Fulcher**

Simply stating the obvious doesn't do this bracelet justice.
The hip mix of rubber and metal, color, and pattern gives this
cuff a contemporary caché.

YOU WILL NEED

- 152 small stainless steel jump rings,
  18 gauge (1.024 mm), 5 mm i.d. (A)

- 10 medium stainless steel jump rings,
  16 gauge (1.291 mm), 6 mm i.d. (B)

- 1 large stainless steel jump ring 14 gauge
  (1.628 mm), 11 mm i.d. (C)

- 56 black rubber O-rings, 16 gauge (1.291 mm),
  8 mm i.d.

- 22 red rubber O-rings, 16 gauge (1.291 mm),
  8 mm i.d.

- 6 inches (15 cm) stainless steel wire

- Flat-nose pliers

- Round-nose pliers

1 | Open the 152 small jump rings (A), close the 10 medium jump rings (B), and close the large jump ring (C).

Note: All jump rings used in steps 2 through 14 are small jump rings (A).

2

Place and close an open jump ring through 4 black O-rings. Repeat, placing and closing another open jump ring through the same 4 black O-rings.

3

Place and close an open jump ring through 2 new black O-rings and 2 black O-rings from step 2. Repeat, placing and closing another open jump ring through the same 4 black O-rings.
Repeat until you have a chain 13 black O-ring pairs long.

4 | Repeat steps 2 and 3 to create a 2nd chain of 13 black O-ring pairs.

5 | Place and close an open jump ring through 2 black O-rings and 2 red O-rings. Repeat with a second jump ring.

6 | Place and close an open jump ring through 2 new red O-rings and the 2 red O-rings from the previous step. Repeat with a second jump ring.
Repeat this step 9 times, until you have a chain starting with a pair of black O-rings and 11 pairs of red O-rings.

7 | Place and close an open jump ring through 2 new black O-rings and the 2 red O-rings on the end of the red and black chain created in step 6. Repeat with a second jump ring.

8 | Place 1 of the all-black chains above the red and black chain.

9

Place and close an open jump ring through the 1st black O-ring pair from the top chain and the 1st black O-ring pair from the bottom chain. Repeat, placing and closing another open jump ring through the 1st black O-ring pair from the top chain and the 1st black O-ring pair from the bottom chain.

Repeat this step 12 times to connect the two chains.

10

Place the second black chain below the red and black chain, aligned as shown.

11 | Repeat step 9 to connect the 3rd chain to the main band.

12 | Place and close an open small jump ring through 4 closed medium jump rings (B).

13

Place and close an open small jump ring through the same 4 closed medium jump rings.

14 | Place and close an open small jump ring through the 2 new closed medium jump rings and 2 closed medium jump rings from the previous step.

15

Place and close an open small jump ring through the same 4 closed medium jump rings in step 14 to create a short chain.

16 | Place and close an open small jump ring through the 2 closed medium jump rings from one end of the short chain and the 2 closed

medium jump rings from the other end of the short chain to form a small triangle.

Repeat, placing and closing another open small jump ring through the same 2 closed medium jump rings from one end of the short chain and the same 2 closed medium jump rings from the other end of the short chain.

17 | Place the small triangle at one end of the main band. Align the triangle and band as shown in step 21.

18 | Place and close an open small jump ring through the top medium jump ring pair of the triangle and the top black O-ring pair from the main band. Repeat, placing and closing another open small jump ring through the same top medium jump ring pair of the triangle and the same top black O-ring pair from the main band.

19 | Place and close an open small jump ring through the top medium jump ring pair of the triangle and the middle black 0-ring pair from the main band. Repeat, placing and closing another open small jump ring through the same top medium jump ring pair of the triangle and the same middle black O-ring pair from the main band.

20 | Place and close an open small jump ring through the bottom medium jump ring pair of the triangle and the middle black 0-ring pair from the main band. Repeat, placing and closing another open small jump ring through the same bottom medium jump ring pair of the triangle and the same middle black O-ring pair from the main band.

21

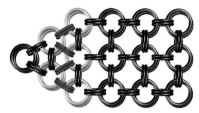

Place and close an open small jump ring through the bottom medium jump ring pair of the triangle and the bottom black O-ring pair from the main band. Repeat, placing and closing another open small jump ring through the same bottom medium jump ring pair of the triangle and the same bottom black O-ring pair from the main band.

22

Use round-nose pliers to bend a small length of stainless steel wire to form a toggle bar as shown.

23

Place and close an open small jump ring through the loop of the toggle bar and the medium jump ring pair from the end of the main band. Repeat, placing and closing another open small jump ring through the loop of the toggle bar and the same medium jump ring (B) pair from the end of the main band.

24

Place and close an open small jump ring through the large jump ring (C) and 2 medium jump rings. Repeat, placing and closing another open small jump ring through the same large jump ring and the same 2 medium jump rings.

Repeat this step to form a small chain, with the large jump ring in the middle.

25

Lay the small chain from Step 24 at the opposite end of the main band, aligned as shown.

26

Repeat steps 18 through 21 to attach the small chain to the main band.

Byzantine Parure

Designed by **Jerry Penner**

This brightly colored parure is worked in the Byzantine or King's Chain pattern. Its intricate-looking design is beautiful in one metal, but becomes more striking when you weave with two colors.

YOU WILL NEED

252 red enameled copper jump rings, 19 gauge (0.9119 mm), 3.175 i.d.

510 half-hard sterling silver jump rings, 19 gauge (0.9119 mm), 3.175 i.d.

Ring marker (page 18)

2 sterling silver lobster clasps

1 pair sterling silver ear wires

Chain-nose pliers

Optional:
Binocular headband magnifiers
Cyanoacrylate glue

BYZANTINE CHAIN PATTERN

1 | Close and mark a ring. This marker ring is not considered part of the repeating pattern.

2 |
Place and close 2 open rings through the closed ring from step 1.

3 |
Place and close 2 open rings through the 2 closed rings from step 2.

4 |
Place and close 2 open rings through the 2 closed rings from step 3.

5 |
Fold the 2 closed rings from step 4 backward as shown.

6 |
Place and close 2 open rings through the 2 closed rings from steps 4 and 5 as shown.

7

Place and close 2 open rings through the 2 closed rings from step 6.

8

Place and close 2 open rings through the 2 closed rings from step 6.

9

Fold the 2 closed rings from step 8 backward as shown.

10

Place and close 2 open rings through the 2 closed rings from steps 8 and 9 as shown. This repeats the positioning of the rings from step 2. To continue the pattern, repeat steps 3 through 10. The Byzantine Chain pattern repeats every 12 links.

Note: To greatly speed construction, open all copper and one half of the silver rings before starting, then close the other half of the silver rings, then add the closed silver rings with the open rings in Steps 3 and 7 as shown and skip steps 4 and 8, as those links will have already been added.

BRACELET

YOU WILL NEED

68 red enameled copper jump rings

140 half-hard sterling silver jump rings.

1 | Use 1 sterling silver ring as the marker ring.

2 | Work the pattern following steps 2 through 10, using red rings in step 2. Repeat the pattern 17 times.

3 |

Finish off the bracelet by adding 3 silver links to the end as shown. The end ring will be the connection point for the lobster clasp. To add a little more stability, you can add a tiny drop of cyanoacrylate glue to the joint in the final ring.

NECKLACE

YOU WILL NEED

164 red enameled copper jump rings

332 half-hard sterling silver jump rings

1 | Use one sterling silver ring as the marker ring.

2 | Work the pattern following steps 2 through 10, using red rings in step 2. Repeat the pattern 41 times.

3 | Finish off the necklace by adding 3 silver links to the end. The end ring will be the connection point for the lobster clasp. To add a little more stability, you can add a tiny drop of cyanoacrylate glue to the joint in the final ring.

EARRINGS

YOU WILL NEED

20 red enameled copper jump rings

38 half-hard sterling silver jump rings

1 | Use 1 sterling silver ring as the marker ring.

2 | Work the pattern following steps 2 through 10.

3 | Repeat the pattern until 10 copper rings have been added to the earring.

4 | Place the ear wire on the marker ring.

5 | Repeat for the second earring.

Crochet Mandala Pendant and Earrings

Designed by **Dylon Whyte**

Elegantly simple or simply elegant—either phrase aptly describes this charming set.

PENDANT

YOU WILL NEED

55 sterling silver jump rings, 21 gauge (0.7239 mm), 2.38 mm i.d. (B)

1 large sterling silver jump ring, 16 gauge

(1.291 mm), 7.14 mm i.d. (A)

11 sterling silver jump rings, 18 gauge (1.024 mm),

3.97 mm i.d. (D)

13 sterling silver jump rings, 21gauge (0.7239 mm), 3.18 mm i.d. (C)

Flat-nose pliers

Leather cord or thin chain

1 | Close 22 jump rings (B).

2 | Open the large jump ring (A).

3 |

Place and close the large open jump ring (A) through the 22 closed jump rings.

4 | Open the remaining 33 jump rings (B).

5 |

Place and close an open jump ring (B) link through any 2 closed jump rings (B) that are attached to the large jump ring.

6 |

Place and close an open jump ring (B) through 2 of the closed jump rings (B) that are attached to the large jump ring (B), including 1 of the jump rings (B) added to in Step 5.

Repeat this step 20 times, until you have added a total of 22 jump rings (B). The final jump ring (B) goes through the 1st jump ring (B) added to in Step 5.

7 | Open 11 jump rings (D) and 13 jump rings (C).

8 |

Place and close an open jump ring (D) through 2 closed jump rings (B) on the edge of the pattern.

9 |

Place and close an open jump ring (C) through 2 closed jump rings (B) on the edge of the pattern, including 1 of the closed jump rings (B) added to in Step 8.

10 |

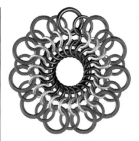

Continue to add alternating jump rings (D) and jump rings (C), with each ring added passing through 2 closed jumps rings (B) on the edge of the pattern, including 1 closed jump ring (B) that the previously added jump ring passed through ,until a total of 22 jump rings (11 jump rings (D) and 11 (C) jump rings) have been added to the edge of the pattern.

11 |

Place and close an open jump ring (B) verti-cally through 2 closed jump rings (C) from the edge of the pattern, so that the jump ring (B) is captured inside (but not passing through) a closed jump ring (D) from the edge of the pattern.
    Repeat this step 11 times.

12 |

Place and close 1 of the remaining jump rings (C) through one of the closed jump rings (D) from the edge of the pattern. Repeat this step, adding a 2nd jump ring (C) to the same closed jump ring (D). This ring is used to attach the pendant to the cord or chain.

13 | Suspend the pendant as desired.

EARRINGS

YOU WILL NEED

160 sterling silver jump rings (spring hard), 21 gauge (0.7239 mm), 2.38 mm i.d. (C)

2 sterling silver jump rings, 16 gauge (1.291 mm), 4.37 mm i.d. (B)

2 sterling silver jump rings, 16 gauge (1.291 mm), 7.14 mm i.d. (A)

Ear wires

Chain-nose pliers

Note: Each earring is composed of three distinct sections: small circle, triangle, and large circle.

Small Circle

1 | Close 34 jump rings (C). Open 1 jump ring (B).

2 |

Place and close the jump ring (B) through 14 closed jump rings (C).

3 | Open 46 jump rings (C).

4 |

Place and close an open jump ring (C) through 1 of the closed jump rings (C) attached to the smaller jump ring.

5 |

Place and close an open jump ring (C) through 2 of the closed jump rings (C) that are attached to the jump ring (B), including the jump ring (C) added to in the previous step.

6 |

Repeating step 5, add 12 more jump rings (C), following the standard European 4-1 pattern.

7 |

Place and close an open jump ring (C) through the closed jump ring (C) that was the final closed jump ring (C) that the final jump ring (C) added in step 5 passed through.
    Sliding the ends of the mail circle together gives you 2 ends, right and left.

Note: You have now completed the small crochet circle that makes up the top part of the earring. You will see that the pattern does not form a complete circle. The next steps explain how to create a small triangle of European 1 in 4 mail that holds the small crochet circle in place.

Joining Triangle

8 | Place and close an open jump ring (C) through the 2 closed jump rings (C) at the left end of the mail circle.

9 | Place and close an open jump ring (C) through the single closed jump ring (C) at the left end of the mail circle.

10 | Place and close an open jump ring (C) through the single closed jump ring (C) at the right end of the mail circle.

11 |

Place and close an open jump ring (C) through the 2 closed jump rings (C) at the right end of the mail circle.

12 | Place and close an open jump ring (C) through the 2 closed jump rings (C) added in steps 8 and 9.

13 | Place and close an open jump ring (C) through the 2 closed jump rings (C) added in steps 9 and 10.

14 |
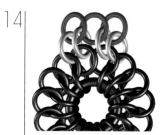
Place and close an open jump ring (C) through the 2 closed jump rings (C) added in steps 11 and 12.

15 | Place and close an open jump ring (C) through the 2 closed jump rings (C) added in steps 12 and 13.

16 | Place and close an open jump ring (C) through the 2 closed jump rings (C) added in steps 13 and 14.

17 |

Place and close an open jump ring (C) through the 2 closed jump rings (C) added in steps 15 and 16. This completes the triangle.

Large Circle

18 | Open 1 jump ring (A).

19 | Place and close the open jump ring (A) through the remaining 20 closed jump rings (C).

20 |

Place and close an open jump ring (C) through 2 closed jump rings (C) that are attached to the jump ring (A).

21 | Place and close an open jump ring (C) through two of the closed jump rings (C) that are attached to the jump ring (A), including one of the jump rings (C) added to in step 20.
  Repeat this step 15 times, until you have added a total of 16 jump rings (C).

22 |

A total of 11 jump rings (C) are on the small circle not attached to the triangle. Starting with the 1st jump ring (C) that is not attached to the triangle, count 4 jump rings (C) around, then take note of the 5th, 6th, and 7th jump rings (C); these will be the jump rings (C) to which the large circle is attached.

23 |

Place and close an open jump ring (C) through the next 2 closed jump rings (C) that complete the edge of the large crochet circle and the jump ring (C) that is the 5th on the bottom of the small circle.

24

Place and close an open jump ring (C) through the next 2 closed jump rings (C) that complete the edge of the large crochet circle and the jump rings (C) that you noted as the 5th and 6th on the bottom of the small circle.

25

Place and close an open jump ring (C) through the next 2 closed jump rings (C) that complete the edge of the large crochet circle and the jump rings (C) that you noted as the 6th and 7th on the bottom of the small circle.

26

Place and close an open jump ring (C) through the next 2 closed jump rings (C) that complete the edge of the large crochet circle and the jump ring (C) that you noted as the 7th on the bottom of the small circle.

27 Place and close an open jump ring (C) through the single closed jump ring (C) at the tip of the triangle that was completed in steps 8 through 17 and through the drop loop of an earring finding.

28

Repeat steps 1 through 27 exactly for the second earring, with one exception. Make sure that the links that you start to add at step 6 are added with an overlap (lean), which is opposite to the overlap (lean) used for the original step 6. This will make the second earring a mirror image of the first.

Free-Form Flat Mail

Designed by **Elizabeth Hake**

Expand your horizons with Elizabeth Hake's version of flat mail. It's a whimsical and one-of-a-kind take on chain mail. Invent your own arrangement and placement of rings.

YOU WILL NEED

Approximately 40 rubber O-rings, ³⁄₃₂", sizes 8-13

193 sterling silver rings, 20 gauge (0.8128 mm), 3 mm i.d.

2"/5cm sterling silver wire, 18 gauge (1.024mm)* or 1 commercial hook or clasp *

Chain-nose

Round-nose pliers

Flush cutting wire snips

Small file

Sheet of paper

Ruler

Pencil

* You may create your own hook or use a commercial one.

1 Arrange the O-rings on a sheet of paper using the photograph as inspiration. Space the rings approximately ³⁄₁₆ inch (5 mm) apart to allow for the chain connections. Place 4 size 9 O-rings to lie along the back of your neck in the arrangement. Once you have made an arrangement, leave the room for a bit (really!). When you come back in, look at your arrangement again and make adjustments as desired. When you're satisfied with the arrangement, lightly trace the outer diameter of each O-ring for reference.

2 Close 61 jump rings. Open 132 jump rings wide enough for you to place them onto an O-ring.

3

Place and close an open jump ring through 2 closed jump rings. Make 4 sets of these chains and set them aside.

4

Start work with the 4 size 9 O-rings that make up the back of the necklace. Place and close an open jump ring through a size 9 O-ring and the end jump ring from 1 of the 3-link chains created in step 3.

5

Place and close an open jump ring through another size 9 O-ring and the other end jump ring of the 3 link chain.

6 | Place and close an open jump ring through 1 of the size 9 O-rings from step 5 and the end jump ring from another 1 of the 3-link chains created in step 3.
   Repeat to create a 2nd pair of connected O-rings.

7 | Place the connected O-rings on the paper pattern. Mark the paper at the places on the pattern where you will want to join the necklace. Some rings are joined in one place; some in two or more places. Marking the pattern will help you remember where to create attachment points.

8 | Place and close an open jump ring through an O-ring and a new closed jump ring, then place and close another open jump ring through the same new closed jump ring and the adjacent O-ring. Work around the pattern, joining all the O-rings at the locations you marked in step 7.

Working Hint: As you join rings, connect them top to bottom first, and then connect rings left to right. You may find that you need to alter your placement from your original design in order to allow the necklace to hang smoothly.

9 | Place and close an open jump ring onto the hook or clasp. Place an open jump ring through the size 9 O-ring at the end of the necklace and the closed jump ring that is attached to the hook or clasp to finish your necklace.

Hana-Gusari Bangle

Designed by **Rachel Dow**

The alternating grid pattern of chain is an elegant addition to a simple silver bangle. The beaded trim is the delicious icing on the cake.

Basic Pattern: **Japanese chain mail, 2-6 pattern**

INTERMEDIATE

YOU WILL NEED

1 sterling silver bangle

82 large sterling silver jump rings, 16 gauge (1.291 mm), 7 mm i.d.

97 small sterling silver jump rings, 18 gauge (1.024 mm), 3.5 mm i.d.

22 sterling silver head pins

22 gemstone beads, 4-5mm

Ring markers (page 18)

Chain-nose pliers

Round-nose pliers

Flush cutting wire snips

1 | Close 40 large jump rings and open 42 large jump rings. Open 97 small jump rings.

2 | Following the instructions on page 15, create 22 head pin and bead combinations.

3 | Place and close an open large jump ring through the loop of each of head pin and bead combination.

4 |

Place and close an open large jump ring through a new closed large jump ring and onto the bangle.
   Repeat this step 19 more times. You will have 20 closed large jump rings on the bangle.

5 |

Bring beside each other 2 of the jump rings added in step 4. Place and close an open small jump ring between the 2 rings.
   Continue around the bangle, attaching the closed large jump rings. You will have a continuous chain of 20 closed large jump rings.

6 | Place a ring marker on any 1 of the 20 closed large jump rings. This becomes the 1st closed large jump ring, and the ring to the right becomes the 2nd closed large jump ring. Count around from the 1st large jump ring and place a temporary marker on the 11th closed large jump.

7 | Place and close an open small jump ring through the 1st closed large jump ring and a new closed large jump ring with bead.

8 | Place and close an open small jump ring through the 2nd closed large jump ring and the closed large jump ring with a bead added in step 7.

9 | Place and close an open small jump ring through the 2nd closed large jump ring and a new closed large jump ring.

10 | Place and close an open small jump ring through the 3rd closed large jump ring and the closed large jump ring added in step 9.

11 | Place and close an open small jump ring through the 3rd closed large jump ring and a new closed large jump ring.

12 | Place and close an open small jump ring through the 4th closed large jump ring and the closed large jump ring added in step 11.

13 | Place and close an open small jump ring through the 4th closed large jump ring and a new closed large jump ring.

14 | Place and close an open small jump ring through the 5th closed large jump ring and the closed large jump ring added in step 13.

15 | Place and close an open small jump ring through the 5th closed large jump ring and a new closed large jump ring.

16 | Place and close an open small jump ring through the 6th closed large jump ring and the closed large jump ring added in step 15.

17 | Place and close an open small jump ring through the 6th closed large jump ring and a new closed large jump ring with bead.

18 |
Place and close an open small jump ring through the 7th closed large jump ring and the closed large jump ring with a bead added in step 17.

19 | Place and close an open small jump ring through the closed large jump ring with a bead added in step 7 and the closed large jump ring added in step 9.

20 | Place and close an open small jump ring through the closed large jump ring added in step 9 and the closed large jump ring added in step 11.

21 | Place and close an open small jump ring through the closed large jump ring added in step 11 and the closed large jump ring added in step 13.

22 | Place and close an open small jump ring through the closed large jump ring added in step 13 and the closed large jump ring added in step 15.

23 |
Place and close an open small jump ring through the closed large jump ring added in step 17 and the closed large jump ring with a bead added in step 17 to complete the 1st row of the 1st triangle.

24 |
Repeat the basic joining process of steps 7 through 23 to add 5 additional rows to the 1st triangle. Use the 1st closed large jump ring with a bead of the preceding row as the starting point for each subsequent row. Each row starts and ends with a closed large jump ring with a bead and has 1 less closed large jump ring than the preceding row (i.e., the 2nd row has 5 closed large jump rings, the 3rd row has 4, the 4th row has 3, the 5th has 2, with a single closed large jump ring with a bead for the 6th and final row).

25 | Repeat steps 10 through 25, starting at the closed large jump ring marked as the 11th in step 6 to complete the 2nd triangle.

26 | Remove the temporary markers to complete the bangle.

Japanese 4-1 Chain Mail Bracelet

Designed by **John Fetvedt**

The small jump rings make this bracelet challenging,

but the delicate end result is well worth the time.

YOU WILL NEED

502 small sterling silver jump rings, 22 gauge
(0.6426 mm), 2.4 mm i.d. (A)

6 sterling silver jump rings, 20 gauge (0.8128 mm),
2 mm i.d. (B)

2 three-ring end bars

1 toggle clasp

Chain-nose pliers

1 | Close 186 small jump rings (A) and open 316
small jump rings (A). Open the 6 large jump
rings (B).

Note: Until step 15, all of the rings in the
following instructions are small jump rings (A).

2 |

Place and close 1 open jump ring through
4 closed jump rings. Repeat, placing and
closing a 2nd open jump ring through the
same 4 closed jump rings.

3 |

Place and close an open jump ring through 2
new closed jump rings and 2 closed jump rings
from the previous step. Repeat, placing and
closing a 2nd open jump ring through the
same closed jump rings.

4 | Repeat step 3 a total of 28 more times to create
a chain that is 31 horizontal ring pairs long.

5 | Repeat steps 2 through 4 twice to create a total
of 3 chains that are each 31 horizontal ring
pairs long.

6 |

Place 2 of the chains side by side so that the
horizontal ring pairs are aligned.

7 |

Place and close an open jump ring through the
1st horizontal ring pair of the top chain and the
1st horizontal ring pair of the bottom chain.
Repeat, placing and closing a 2nd open jump
ring through the same closed jump rings.

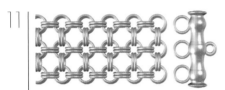

8 | Place and close an open jump ring through the 2nd horizontal ring pair of the top chain and the 2nd horizontal ring pair of the bottom chain. Repeat, placing and closing a 2nd open jump ring through the same closed jump rings.

9 | Repeat step 8 a total of 29 more times, until both chains are connected.

10 | Align the linked chains with the 3rd chain, so that the horizontal ring pairs are aligned. Repeat Steps 7 through 9 to connect the three chains.

11 |

Place 1 of the end bars at 1 end of the connected chains.

12 | Place and close an open jump ring through the top ring of the end bar and the top horizontal ring pair of the connected chain. Repeat, placing and closing a 2nd open jump ring through the same closed jump rings and top ring of the end bar.

13 |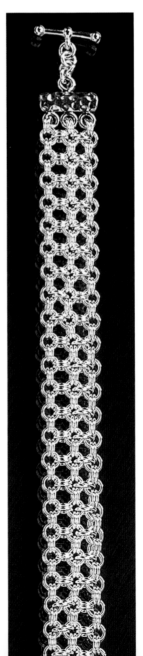

Repeat step 12 twice to join the chain to the end bar.

14 | Repeat steps 11 through 13 with the opposite end of the chain and the end bar.

15 | Place and close an open jump ring (B) through the single bar end loop.

16 | Place and close an open jump ring (B) through the jump ring (B) added in step 15.

17 |

Place and close an open jump ring (B) through the jump ring (B) added in step 16 and the loop of one side of the toggle clasp.

18 | Repeat steps 15 through 17 with the other bar end and other side of the toggle clasp.

Lace Mail Cocktail Collar with Pearls

Designed by **2-Roses**

This bold collar design is transformed into something feminine with the addition of freshwater pearls. It longs to be paired with a little black dress.

Basic Pattern: European 6-1

INTERMEDIATE

YOU WILL NEED

- 24 large nickel silver jump rings, 16 gauge (1.291 mm), 9 mm i.d. (A)

- 430 medium nickel silver jump rings, 16 gauge (1.291 mm), 6 mm i.d. (B)

- 77 small nickel silver jump rings, 16 gauge (1.291 mm), 3 mm i.d. (C)

- 24 fully drilled freshwater pearls, 2 x 3 mm

- 24 Head pins

- Toggle clasp

- Flat-nose pliers

- Needle-nose pliers

- Round-nose pliers

- Flush cutting wire snips

- Optional:
    - Patina solution
    - Cotton swabs

1 | Open 190 medium jump rings (B), close 240 medium jump rings (B), and open the 24 large jump rings (A).
   Open 53 small jump rings (C) and close 24 small jump rings (C).

2 |

Place and close an open medium jump ring (B) through 6 closed medium jump rings.

3

Place and close an open medium jump ring through 2 new closed medium jump rings and 4 closed medium jump rings from step 2.

4 | Repeat step 3 a total of 115 more times, until you have a chain that is 119 edge rings and 117 internal rings in length.

5

Place and close an open medium jump ring through 4 closed medium jump rings on 1 end of the chain.
   Repeat this step at the opposite end of the chain.

6
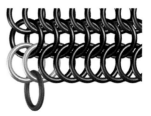
Starting at either end of the chain, place and close an open medium jump ring through the 1st and 2nd closed medium jump rings on the edge of the chain.

7 | Place and close an open medium jump ring through the 2nd and 3rd closed medium jump rings on the edge of the chain.

8 | Place and close an open medium jump ring through the 3rd and 4th closed medium jump rings on the edge of the chain.

9 | Skip the 5th closed medium jump ring on the edge of the chain. Place and close an open medium jump ring through the 1st and 2nd closed medium rings on the edge of the chain that follow the 5th.

10 | Repeat steps 7 through 9. You will continue to add groups of 3 medium jump rings to the edge of the chain, skipping every 5th edge ring to keep the groups separate. There will be a total of 24 groups of 3 medium rings on the edge of the chain.

11 | Place and close an open large jump ring (A) through a set of 3 medium jump rings (B) added in steps 6 through 8.

12 | Repeat step 11 a total of 23 more times, adding large jump rings to each group of 3 medium jump rings.

13 | Place and close an open small jump ring (C) through the medium jump ring added in step 7 and a new closed small jump ring.

14 | Repeat step 13 a total of 23 more times, for the middle jump ring of each group of 3 medium jump rings (B) on the edge of the chain.

Note: If desire, apply patina solution to the necklace at this point, before adding the pearls. Dab patina solution onto the head pins and connecting rings with a cotton swab after they are attached to the necklace.

15 | Place all of the drilled freshwater pearls on head pins. Create a wrapped bead loop for each head pin (see page 15).

16 | Place and close an open small jump ring (C) through a headpin loop and the small closed jump ring added in step 13.

17 | Repeat step 16 once for each of the small closed jump rings added in step 14.

18 | Place and close an open small jump ring through the medium jump ring added in step 5. Repeat, placing and closing another open small jump ring through the same medium jump ring added in step 5.

19 | Place and close an open small jump ring through the 2 small jump rings added in step 18 and the lead chain of the bar end of the toggle clasp.

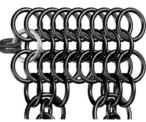

20 | Place and close an open small jump ring through the medium jump ring added in step 5 and the large loop end of the toggle clasp. Repeat, placing and closing another open small jump ring through the same medium jump ring added in step 5 and the large loop end of the toggle clasp.

Flexible Chain Mail Watchband

Designed by **Andrew Telesca**

Mix solid, metal rings with neoprene O-rings to create a flexible chain mail band. The smaller metal rings are the workhorses in this pattern because you attach multiple rings to a single closed ring.

Basic Pattern: Japanese chain mail, 12-2 variation

INTERMEDIATE

YOU WILL NEED

18 mm rectangular watch face

208 stainless steel jump rings, 20 gauge (0.8128 mm), 3 mm i.d. (A)

2 large stainless steel jump rings, 16 gauge (1.291 mm), 9.5 mm i.d. (B)

41 neoprene O-rings, 8 mm i.d.

8 inches(20 cm), 22 gauge (0.6426mm) stainless steel wire

Flat-nose pliers

Flush cutting wire snips

3.97 mm mandrel or #7 knitting needle

Note: The neoprene and stainless steel band measures approximately 5¾ inches (15 cm) in length, suitable for a small wrist. The total number of rings required will depend on the wrist measurement of wearer, the number of rings used in this project will make a watchband suitable for a woman's wrist.

1 | Open 204 small jump rings (A) and close 4 small jump rings (A). Open the 2 large jump rings (B).

Note: Only small jump rings and O-rings are used to construct the band.

2 | Place and close a small open jump ring (A) through 2 O-rings. Place and close a 2nd open jump ring through the same 2 O-rings.

3 | Place and close an open jump ring through a new O-ring and an O-ring from the previous step. Repeat, placing and closing another open jump ring through the same 2 O-rings.

4 | Repeat steps 2 and 3 a total of 11 times, until you have a chain that is 14 O-rings long. Set this chain aside.

5 | Repeat steps 2 through 4, making a second chain 14 O-rings long. Set this chain aside.

6 | Repeat steps 2 through 4, except repeat steps 2 and 3 a total of 10 more times during step 4, making a chain that is 13 O-rings long.

7 |

Align 1 of the 14-O-ring chains above the 13-O-ring chain.

8 |

Place and close an open jump ring through the 1st O-ring of the top chain and the 1st O-ring of the bottom chain. Repeat with a 2nd ring.

9 |

Place and close an open jump ring through the 2nd O-ring of the top chain and the 1st O-ring of the bottom chain. Repeat with a second ring.

10 | Repeat steps 8 and 9 a total of 13 times to attach both chains.

11 |

Align the remaining 14-O-ring chain below the 13-O-ring chain.

12 |

Place and close an open jump ring through the 1st O-ring of the middle chain and the 1st O-ring of the bottom chain. Repeat with a 2nd ring.

13 |

Place and close an open jump ring through the 1st O-ring of the middle chain and the 2nd O-ring of the bottom chain. Repeat with a 2nd ring.

14 | Repeat steps 12 and 13 across the length of the chain.

15 |

Place and close an open jump ring through the 1st O-ring of the top chain and 2 new closed jump rings. Repeat, placing and closing another open jump ring through the same O-ring and the same closed jump rings.

16 |

Place and close an open jump ring through the 1st O-ring of the middle chain and the 2 closed jump rings added in step 15. Repeat, placing and closing another open jump ring through the same O-ring and the same closed jump rings.

17 |

Place and close an open jump ring through the 1st O-ring of the bottom chain and the 2 closed jump rings added in step 16. Repeat, placing and closing another open jump ring through the same O-ring and the same closed jump rings.

18 | Repeat steps 15 through 17 at the opposite end of the chain to complete the watchband. Set the completed band aside.

19 | With chain-nose pliers, carefully grip one end of a watchface pin, then push back and remove the pin from its hole. Keep a good grip on the pin with the pliers so that it doesn't go flying across the room. Remove the 2nd pin in the same way.

20 | Cut the 22 gauge stainless steel wire in half. Make a coil of 20 wraps on the mandrel or knitting needle with each wire.

Note: Larger and smaller watch faces will require coils with either a greater or fewer number of wraps.

21 | Carefully bend the coil apart between the 5th and 6th wraps (see photo). Bend it just enough to make it easy to slip the large jump ring (B) into the space. Make a 2nd bend between the 15th and 16th wraps.

22 | Place and close an open large jump ring (B) through the center 10 wraps of the coil.

23 | Slip the pin into the coil. If needed, remove the coil to trim the coil ends.
    Make sure to make the cuts on the bottom side of the coil and where they won't be visible.

24 | Replace the pin, covered by the coil and large jump ring (B), back into the watch face.

25 | Repeat steps 20 through 24 for the other side of the watch face.

26

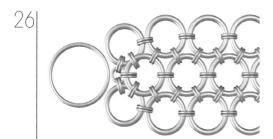

Set the watch face with the large jump ring (B) at the end of the watchband as shown.

27

Place and close an open small jump ring through the large jump ring and the top O-ring of the watchband. Repeat, placing and closing another open small jump ring through the same large jump ring and the same O-ring.

28

Place and close an open small jump ring through the large jump ring and the pair of closed small jump rings added in steps 15 through 17. Repeat, placing and closing another open small jump ring through the same large jump ring and the same pair of closed small jump rings.

29

Place and close an open small jump ring through the large jump ring and the bottom O-ring of the watchband. Repeat, placing and closing another open small jump ring through the same large jump ring and the same O-ring.
    Repeat steps 22 through 25 to attach the opposite end of the band to the watch face.

Japanese 6-1 Chain Mail Bracelet

Designed by **John Fetvedt**

This variation of a Japanese chain mail pattern uses three connecting rings rather than one.

YOU WILL NEED

26 large sterling silver jump rings, 14 gauge (1.628 mm), 10 mm i.d.

147 small sterling silver jump rings, 16 gauge (1.291 mm), 4 mm i.d.

2 foldover or lobster clasps

Chain-nose pliers

Finished length: Approximately 6½"/17cm

1 | Close 24 large jump rings. Open 147 small jump rings. Open 2 large jump rings (A).

2 | Place and close an open large jump ring through the loop of a foldover or lobster clasp. Repeat with the 2nd clasp.

3 | Place and close an open small jump ring through 2 closed large jump rings. Repeat twice, placing and closing 2 open small jump rings through the same 2 closed large jump rings.

4 | Place and close an open small jump ring through a new closed large jump ring and a closed large jump ring from the previous step. Repeat twice, placing and closing 2 open small jump rings through the same 2 closed large jump rings.

5 | Repeat step 4 a total of 9 times, until you have a chain that is 12 large jump rings in length.

6 | Place and close an open small jump ring through one of the large jump rings with a clasp

and a closed large jump ring from the end of the chain completed in step 5. Repeat twice, placing and closing 2 open small jump rings trough the same 2 closed large jump rings.

7 | Repeat steps 2 through 6 to complete a 2nd chain that has a total of 13 closed large jump rings and a clasp.

8 | Place the 2 chains side by side, with the clasps at the same end, offset as in figure 5.

9 | Place and close an open small jump ring through the 1st large jump ring of each chain. Repeat twice, placing and closing, in turn, 2 open small jump rings through the same 2 closed large jump rings.

10 | Place and close an open small jump ring through the 1st large jump ring of the bottom chain and the 2nd large jump ring of the top chain. Repeat twice, placing and closing, in turn, 2 open small jump rings through the same 2 closed large jump rings.

11 | Repeat steps 9 and 10, until all of the closed large jump rings from both chains are connected.

Japanese
Lace Collar

Designed by **Anne Kelly**

The sinuous drape of this dense collar makes it a pleasure to wear. Many small rings make it a challenging but not unconquerable project.

YOU WILL NEED

1002 sterling silver jump rings, 21 gauge,
2.38 mm i.d. (A)

148 sterling silver jump rings, 19 gauge,
3.57 mm i.d. (B)

144 sterling silver jump rings, 19 gauge,
3.97 mm i.d. (C)

142 sterling silver jump rings, 19 gauge,
4.37 mm i.d. (D)

1 silver sterling silver ring, 16 gauge, 4.37 mm i.d (E)*

1 sterling silver 13.5mm lobster claw clasp

Chain-nose pliers

* This is your clasp ring. For best results, use a soldered jump ring.

Note: Don't let our simplified illustrations fool you—all the rings depicted in this project from step 14 onward are actually doubled rings, not single. You create three chains composed of double rings.

1 | Open the1002 jump rings (A), close 146 jump rings (B), open 2 jump rings (B), close the 144 jump rings (C) and close the 142 jump rings (D).

To create the first chain:

2 | Place and close an open jump ring (A) through 4 closed jump rings (B).

3 |

Place and close an open jump ring (A) through the same 4 closed jump rings (B) as in step 2.

4 |

Place and close an open jump ring (A) through 2 closed jump rings (B) and 2 new closed jump rings (B) from the previous step. Repeat, placing and closing a 2nd open jump ring through the same 4 closed jump rings.

5 | Repeat Step 4 a total of 35 times. Set the chain aside. Mark it as chain 1.

To create the second chain:

6 | Place and close an open jump ring (A) through 4 closed jump rings (C).

7 | Place and close an open jump ring (A) through the same 4 closed jump rings (C) as in step 6.

8 | Place and close an open jump ring (A) through 2 closed jump rings (C) and 2 of the closed jump rings (C) from the previous step. Repeat, placing and closing a 2nd open jump ring through the same 4 closed jump rings.

9 | Repeat step 8 a total of 69 times, until you have a chain that is a total of 72 closed jump ring pairs (C) in length. Set the chain aside. Mark it as chain 2.

To create the third chain:

10 | Place and close an open jump ring (A) through 4 closed jump rings (D).

11 | Place and close an open jump ring (A) through the same 4 closed jump rings (D) as in step 10.

12 | Place and close an open jump ring (A) through 2 closed jump rings (D) and 2 of the closed jump rings (D) from the previous step. Repeat, placing and closing a 2nd open jump ring through the same 4 closed jump rings.

13 | Repeat step 12 a total of 68 times, until you have a chain that is a total of 71 closed jump ring pairs (D) in length. Set the chain aside. Mark it as chain 3.

14 |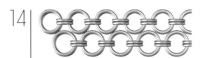

Place chain 2 below chain 1 aligned so that the 1st closed jump ring pair (C) of chain 2 sits between the 1st and 2nd pairs of closed jump rings (B) of chain 1.

15 |

Place and close an open jump ring (A) through the 1st pair of closed jump rings (B) of chain 1 and the 1st closed jump ring pair (C) of chain 2. Repeat, placing and closing a 2nd open jump ring through the same 4 closed jump rings.

16 |

Place and closed an open jump ring (A) through the 2nd closed jump ring pair (B) chain 1 and the 1st closed jump ring pair (C) of chain 2. Repeat, placing and closing a 2nd open jump ring through the same 4 closed jump rings.

17 | Repeat Steps 15 and 16 with the closed jump ring pairs (B) from chain 1 and the closed jump ring pairs (C) from chain 2, until both chains are connected.

18 |

Place chain 3 below the connected chains, aligned so that the 1st closed jump ring pair (D) of chain 3 sits between the 1st and 2nd closed jump ring pairs (C) of chain 2, as shown.

19 | Place and close an open jump ring (A) through the 1st closed jump ring pair (C) of chain 2 and the 1st closed jump ring pair (D) of chain 3. Repeat, placing and closing a 2nd open jump ring through the same 4 closed jump rings.

20 | Place and close an open jump ring (A) through the 2nd closed jump ring pair (C) of chain 2 and the 1st closed jump ring pair (D) of the chain 3. Repeat, placing and closing a 2nd open jump ring through the same 4 closed jump rings.

21 | Repeat Steps 19 and 20 with the closed jump ring pairs (C) from chain 2 and the closed jump ring pairs (D) from chain 3, until both chains are completely connected.

22 | Place and close an open jump ring (B) through the soldered clasp ring (E). Repeat, placing and closing a 2nd open jump ring through the same 4 closed jump rings.

23 | Place and close an open jump ring (A) through the 1st pair of closed jump rings (B) from the end of chain 1 and the pair of closed jump rings (B) from the previous step. Repeat, placing and closing a 2nd open jump ring through the same 4 closed jump rings.

24 | Place and close an open jump ring (A) through the loop or ring of the lobster clasp and the 73rd pair of closed jump rings (B) from the other end of chain 1. Repeat, placing and closing a 2nd open jump ring through the same 4 closed jump rings.

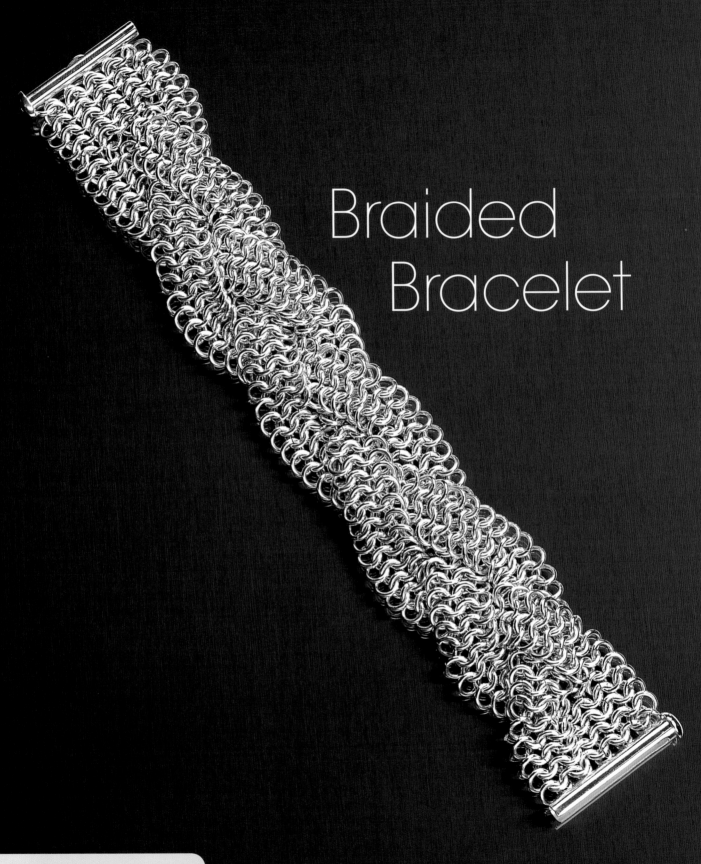

Braided
Bracelet

Designed by **Stephanie Morton**

Make three separate strands of sterling silver chain mail, then artfully braid them to create a glistening showstopper of a bracelet.

YOU WILL NEED

742 sterling silver jump rings, 18 gauge (1.024 mm), 3.25 mm i.d.

1 commercial 5-ring bracelet tube clasp

Chain-nose pliers

Optional:
Binocular headband magnifiers (see page 10)
3.25 mm mandrel
Jewelry saw and blade
Tumbler and polishing material

Finished length: approximately 7 inches (18 cm)

1 | Open 376 jump rings and close 366 jump rings.

2 | Following the instructions for chainlets on page 18, create 3 strands of European 4-1 chain mail, 3 rows wide, that have a total of 52 edge jump rings each.

3 |

Place and close an open jump ring through 2 new closed jump rings and 2 closed jump rings on the end of 1 of the 3 strands. This creates a strand 53 edge rings and 52 center rings in length.

4 |

Place and close an open jump ring through the 2 closed jump rings added in step 3 to create a strand that is 53 edge rings and 53 center rings in length.

5 | Repeat steps 3 and 4 with the remaining 2 strands.

6 | Lay the 3 strands vertically, side by side.

7 |

Place and close a 4th row of 53 open jump rings down the left edge of the 1st and 2nd strands.

8 |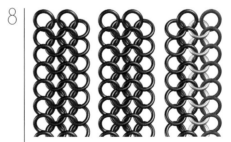

Place and close a 4th row of 53 open jump rings down the right edge of the 3rd strand. Note how this strand is now a mirror image of the first 2 strands. Set the strands aside.

9 | Following the instructions for chainlets on page 18, create 2 rectangles of European 4-1 chain mail. Each rectangle should be made of 11 rows, 4 edge jump rings in width.

10 |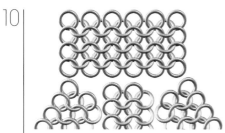

Place the 1st, 2nd ,and 3rd strands, in order, below 1 of the rectangles, aligned as shown.

11 | Place and close an open jump ring through the top 2 closed jump rings of the 1st strand and the 1st and 2nd closed jump rings on the bottom of 1 of the rectangles made in step 9.

12 | Place and close an open jump ring through the top 2 closed jump rings of the 2nd strand and the 3rd and 4th closed jump rings on the bottom of the rectangle.

13 |

Place and close an open jump ring through the top 2 closed jump rings of the 3rd strand and the 5th and 6th closed jump rings on the bottom of the rectangle.

14 |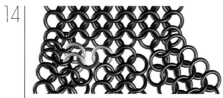

Reopen the top closed jump ring from the right side of the 1st strand, place it through the top closed jump ring from the left side of the 2nd strand, and reclose, as shown.

15 |

Reopen the top closed jump ring from the left side of the 3rd strand, place it through the top closed jump ring from the right side of the 2nd strand , and reclose, as shown.

16 | Braid the 3 strands together: 1st strand over the 2nd, 3rd strand over the 1st, 2nd strand over the 3rd. Repeat the braiding sequence along the strands, finishing with the 1st strand over the 2nd. When you finish note that the 3rd strand is now in the first position, the 1st strand in the 2nd position, and the 2nd strand in the 3rd position.

17 |

Place the 2nd rectangle below the 3 strands, aligned as shown.

18 | Place and close an open jump ring through the bottom 2 closed jump rings of the 1st strand and the 1st and 2nd closed jump rings on the top of the rectangle.

19 | Place and close an open jump ring through the bottom 2 closed jump rings of the 2nd strand and the 3rd and 4th closed jump rings on the top of the rectangle.

20 |

Place and close an open jump ring through the bottom 2 closed jump rings of the 3rd strand and the 5th and 6th closed jump rings on the top of the rectangle.

21

Reopen the bottom closed jump ring from the right side of the 1st strand, place it through the bottom closed jump ring from the left side of the 2nd strand, and reclose, as shown.

22

Reopen the bottom closed jump ring from the left side of the 3rd strand, place it through the bottom closed jump ring from the right side of the 2nd strand, and reclose, as shown.

23

Place and close an open jump ring through the 1st and 2nd closed jump rings from the right end of the chain.

24

Repeat step 23 four more times, placing and closing open jump rings through the 2nd and 3rd, 3rd and 4th, 4th and 5th, and 5th and 6th jump rings from the right end of the chain.

25

Align one half of the slide clasp with the right end of the chain.

26

Place and close a total of 6 open jump rings through the row of 5 jump rings added to the end of the chain and the 5 loops of the slide clasp, as shown.

27 Repeat steps 23 through 26 on the opposite end of the chain, making sure that the clasp is aligned properly.

28 If desired, join the strands in 2 or 3 places with open jump rings. If you plan on tumbling the bracelet, place extra holder rings to keep the strands from unbraiding.

Chandelier Earrings

Designed by **Rachel Dow**

These earrings rightly earn the *nom de bijoux* "chandelier." The circular shapes of the earrings are held in place by attaching the chainmail through drilled silver discs.

YOU WILL NEED

164 small sterling silver jump rings, 20 gauge (0.8128 mm), 3.5 mm i.d. (A)

2 sterling silver discs, 24 gauge (0.5106 mm), 16 mm diameter

20 large sterling silver jump rings, 20 gauge (0.8128 mm), 5 mm i.d. (B)

44 gemstone beads, 2-3 mm

44 sterling silver head pins

2 sterling silver ear wires

Fine point permanent marker

Center punch

Hammer

Drill

#65 (0.889 mm) drill bit

Chain-nose pliers

Round-nose pliers

Flush cutting wire snips

1 | Arrange 12 of the small rings evenly spaced around one disc. At each ring, make a small mark on the disc, approximately 1/16 inch (1.6 mm) from the edge. Use the center punch to dimple the marks on the discs. Drill each mark with the #65 drill bit. Repeat with the second disc, using the first disc as a template, if you wish.

2 | Open 104 small rings (A). Close 60 small rings (A). Open the 20 large rings (B) Prepare 44 head pin and bead combinations (see page 15).

3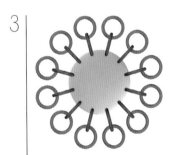

Place an open small ring through 1 of the holes on the disc, place a closed small ring onto the open ring, and close the open ring as shown. Repeat this step for the 11 remaining holes.

4

Place an open small ring through 2 of the closed edge links added in step 3. Place the loop of a head pin and bead combination onto the open ring and close the open ring, making sure that the head pin and bead combination is on the outside of the pattern as shown. Repeat this step 11 times to complete the 1st row.

5

Place an open small ring through 1 of the horizontal edge rings from the first row. (Note: The correct rings can be identified as the edge rings that do not have head pin and bead combinations attached to them and are attached to 3 vertical rings.) Place a closed small ring onto the open ring and close the open ring.

6

Place and close an open small ring through a horizontal edge ring that is beside the horizontal edge ring that was added to in step 5 and through the closed ring that was added in step 5 as shown.

Repeat this step 5 times for the remaining horizontal edge rings, making sure that only 1 ring is added to each horizontal edge ring, as shown.

7

Place an open small ring through 2 of the closed edge links added in step 5. Place the loop of a head pin and bead combination onto the open ring and close the open ring, making sure that the head pin and bead combination is on the outside of the pattern as in figure 6. Repeat this step 5 times to complete the 2nd row. The pattern is now tapering into a cone shape hanging below the disc.

8

Place an open small ring through 1 of the horizontal edge rings from the 2nd row. Place a closed small ring onto the open ring and close the open ring.

9

Place and close an open small ring through a horizontal edge ring that is beside the horizontal edge ring added in step 8 and through the closed ring that was added in step 7.

Repeat steps 8 and 9 two times for the remaining horizontal edge rings, making sure that only 1 ring is added to each horizontal edge ring.

10 | Place an open small ring through 2 of the closed edge links added in steps 8 and 9. Place the loop of a head pin and bead combination onto the open ring and close the open ring, making sure that the head pin and bead combination is on the outside of the pattern as shown. Repeat this step 2 times to complete the third row.

11 | Place an open small ring through the 3 end rings. Place the loop of a headpin and bead combination onto the open ring and close the open ring. This completes the bottom half of the earring.

12 | Working on the other side of the disc, place an open large ring through 2 of the small rings that are attached to the disc. Place a closed small ring onto the open large ring and close the open large ring. Repeat this step 5 times, as shown.

13 | Place an open large ring through 2 of the small closed rings added in step 12. Place a closed small ring onto the open large ring and close the open large ring. Repeat this step 2 times, making sure that only one ring is added to each small closed ring.

14 | Place an open large ring through the 3 small closed rings added in step 13. Place an ear wire on to the large open ring and close.

15 | Repeat steps 3 through 14 to make the matching earring.

C
Ca
Amul

Designed by **Rachel Dow**

Making a coif is a traditional technique used by armorers to create a circular form. This adaptation encloses a special stone, bead, or ceramic shard in a sterling silver cage to keep close to your heart. Adorning the cages with gemstone beads is an optional addition.

YOU WILL NEED

- 142 large sterling silver jump rings, 20 gauge (0.8128 mm), 5 mm i.d. (A)
- 180 small sterling silver jump rings, 20 gauge (0.8128 mm), 3.5 mm i.d. (B)
- 2 tumbled stones or large beads, 10 mm
- 1 tumbled stone or large bead, 30 mm
- 30 sterling silver head pins (optional)
- 30 gemstone beads, 3mm (optional)
- 1 sterling silver bail finding
- Leather necklace strand with clasp
- Sterling silver ear wires
- Chain-nose pliers
- Round-nose pliers
- Flush cutting wire snips

PENDANT/AMULET

1

Refer to the instructions on page 18 to create European 4-1 chainlets. Use large jump rings (A) to create a rectangle of European 4-1 chain mail that is 15 outer edge rings wide by 8 rows high.

2

Bring the edges of the rectangle around and join them together using 4 open large rings to form a tube, as shown.

3

Place and close an open large ring through 2 edge links.

4

Place and close an open large ring through 3 edge links, including 1 of the edge links from step 3.

5 |

Repeat steps 3 and 4 until you have added a total of 10 large rings to the edge of the tube, 5 that go through 2 edge rings and 5 that go through 3 edge rings, alternating.

6 |

Place and close an open large ring through the 10 rings added in steps 3 through 5.

7 | Place the 30 mm tumbled stone or bead inside of the closed tube.

8 |

Place and close 5 open large rings through 3 edge rings each, as shown.

9 |

Place and close 5 open large rings through the 5 rings added in step 8, as shown.

10 |

Place and close an open large ring through the 5 rings added in step 9, as shown.

11 | Attach the finished coif cage to a necklace bail and string onto the leather necklace strand.

12 | If desired, add gemstone beads to your amulet pendant with headpin and bead combinations (see page 15). The pendant shown has 8 beads randomly attached to the coif cage.

EARRINGS

1 |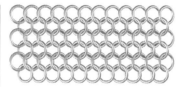

Use small jump rings (B) to create a rectangle of European 4-1 chain mail that is 12 outer edge rings wide by 6 rows high.

2 |

Bring the edges of the rectangle around and join them together using 3 open small rings to form a tube, as shown.

3 |

Place and close an open small ring through 2 edge links.

4

Place and close an open small ring through 3 edge links, including 1 of the edge links from step 3.

5

Repeat steps 3 and 4 until you have added a total of 8 small rings to the edge of the tube, 4 that go through 2 edge rings and 4 that go through 3 edge rings, alternating.

6

Place and close an open small ring through the 8 rings added in steps 3 through 5.

7 Place a small tumbled stone or bead inside of the closed tube.

8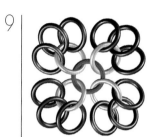

Place and close 4 open small rings through 3 edge rings each, as shown.

9

Place an open small ring through all 4 rings added in Step 9, as shown. Before closing this small ring, add an ear wire to finish the earring.
   Repeat Steps 1 through 9 to make a 2nd earring.

10 If desired, add gemstone beads to your earrings with head pin and bead combinations (see page 15). Each earring shown has 7 beads randomly attached to the coif cage.

Diamond Chain Mail Earrings

Designed by **John Fetvedt**

Diamonds are a girl's best friend! These simple, geometric forms are the perfect introduction to creating shapes by increasing and decreasing the number of rings per row. The ring size makes these earrings a challenge.

ADVANCED

YOU WILL NEED

200 gold filled jump rings, 22 gauge (0.6426 mm), 2.4 mm i.d.

Ring marker (see page 18)

2 ear wires

Chain-nose pliers

Optional:
Binocular headband magnifiers (see page 10)
Tumbler and polishing material (see page 11)

1 | Open 99 rings.

2 |

Row 1: Close 1 jump ring and thread a ring marker through it to mark the start of the pattern.

3 |

Row 2: Place 2 open rings through the first ring. Close these rings.

4 |
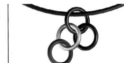
Row 3: Place an open ring through the 1st ring on the left of row 2. Close this ring.

Place an open ring through the 1st and 2nd rings of row 2. Close this ring.

Place an open ring through the last ring of row 2. Close this ring to complete row 3.

Note: The pattern is beginning to form a triangle of alternating rows, with the high side of the 1st row to the left, the high side of the 2nd row to the right, and the high side of the 3rd row to the left.

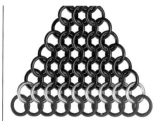

5 | Rows 4-10: Continue adding rings as in step 4 to form alternating rows until you have a row that is 10 rings wide.

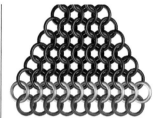

6 | To decrease the size of the following rows, do *not* add a ring through only the 1st ring of row 10. Instead, place and close an open ring through the 1st and 2nd rings of row 10, then an open ring through the 2nd and 3rd rings, and so on to the end of the row. Do *not* close a ring through only the last ring of row 10. This adds a total of 9 rings to row 11.

7 | Rows 12-19: Add rows of decreasing length until the last row consists of only a single ring.

8 | Remove the ring marker from step 1 and attach an ear wire to that ring.

9 | Follow steps 1 through 7 and complete an identical second earring. To make the 2nd earring a mirror image of the 1st, attach the ear wire to the final ring added in step 7. Remove the ring marker added in step 1.

Double Strand Japanese Cube Necklace

Designed by **Rachel Dow**

Move your chain mail into the third dimension with these cubes of Japanese-style mail. Choose a special focus bead—a carved semiprecious gemstone or a handmade lampwork—for a one-of-a-kind necklace.

ADVANCED

YOU WILL NEED

288 gold-filled small jump rings, 16 gauge (1.291 mm), 3.5 mm i.d. (A)

198 gold-filled large jump rings, 18 gauge (1.024 mm), 5 mm i.d. (B)

2 gold-filled head pins

2 focus beads, 12-13mm

1 gold-filled two-strand slide clasp

Chain nose pliers

Round nose pliers

Flush cutters

Ring marker (see page 18)

1 | Open 218 small jump rings (A), close 70 small jump rings (A), open 10 large jump rings (B), and close 188 large jump rings (B). Set the large jump rings aside until step 36. Small jump rings are used in steps 2 through 35.

2 |
Place and close an open jump ring (A) through 2 closed jump rings (A).

3 |
Place and close an open jump ring through a new closed jump ring and one closed jump ring from the previous step.

4 | Repeat step 3 a total of 6 more times to create a chain that is 9 horizontal jump rings in length.

5 |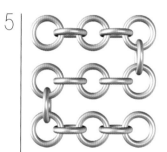
Fold the chain back on itself twice, aligned as shown.

6 | Place and close an open jump ring through the 1st and 6th closed horizontal jump rings.

7 | Place and close an open jump ring through the 2nd and 5th closed horizontal jump rings.

8 | Place and close an open jump ring through the 5th and 8th closed horizontal jump rings.

9 |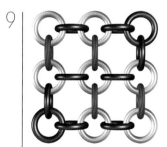
Place and close an open jump ring through the 4th and 9th closed horizontal jump rings to complete a small square of Japanese 4-2 pattern chain mail.

Place a ring marker on each corner of the small square. Mark the top of the small square: all additions will be made on the top.

Note: The small square consists of 9 horizontal jump rings and 12 vertical jump rings. The vertical jump rings are also divided into rows of 2 and 3 jump rings. In the rows of 2 jump rings, the vertical jump rings are parallel to each other, and in the rows of 3 jump rings, the vertical jump rings are perpendicular to each other. All attachments for turning the square into a cube are made to vertical jump rings.

10

Place and close an open jump ring through a new closed jump ring and the 1st vertical closed jump ring from the small square.

11

Place and close an open jump ring through a new closed jump ring and the 2nd vertical closed jump ring from the small square.

Note: Make sure that the closed jump rings added in steps 10 and 11 are folded to the inside, as in both steps 10 and 11.

12

Place and close an open jump ring through the 3rd vertical closed jump ring and the closed horizontal jump ring added in step 10.

13

Place and close an open jump ring through the 4th vertical closed jump ring and the 2 closed horizontal jump rings added in steps 10 and 11.

14

Place and close an open jump ring through the 5th vertical closed jump ring and the closed horizontal jump ring added in step 11.

15

Place and close an open jump ring through a new closed jump ring, the 6th vertical closed jump ring, and the closed horizontal jump ring added in step 10.

16

Place and close an open jump ring through a new closed jump ring, the 7th vertical closed jump ring and the closed horizontal jump ring added in step 11.

Note: Make sure that the closed jump rings added in steps 15 and 16 are folded to the inside.

17

Place and close an open jump ring through the 8th vertical closed jump ring and the closed horizontal jump ring added in step 15.

18

Place and close an open jump ring through the 9th vertical closed jump ring and the 2 closed horizontal jump rings added in steps 15 and 16.

19

Place and close an open jump ring through the 10th vertical closed jump ring and the closed horizontal jump ring added in step 16.

20

Place and close an open jump ring through the 11th vertical closed jump ring and the closed horizontal jump ring added in step 15.

21

Place and close an open jump ring through the 12th vertical closed jump ring and the closed horizontal jump ring added in step 16.

Note: The top of the small square now consists of 4 horizontal jump rings and 12 vertical jump rings. The vertical jump rings are still divided into rows of 2 and 3 jump rings. However, in the rows of 2 jump rings, the vertical jump rings are now perpendicular to each other; in the rows of 3 jump rings, the vertical jump rings are now parallel to each other.

22

Place and close an open jump ring through 2 new closed jump rings and the 1st vertical closed jump ring. Make sure that the closed jump rings are folded, one to the left and one to the right.

23

Place and close an open jump ring through a new closed jump ring, the 2nd vertical closed jump ring, and the closed jump ring added in step 22 that is folded to the right. Make sure that the closed jump added in this step is folded to the right. Place a ring marker on the closed jump ring added during this step.

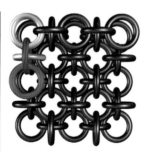

24

Place and close an open jump ring through a new closed jump ring, the 3rd vertical closed jump ring, and the left closed jump ring that was added in step 22.

25

Place and close an open jump ring through a new closed jump ring, the 4th vertical closed jump ring, and the right closed jump ring that was added in step 22.

26

Place and close an open jump ring through a closed jump ring, the 5th vertical closed jump ring and the closed jump ring added in step 23.

27

Place and close an open jump ring through the 6th vertical closed jump ring and the 2 closed jump rings added in steps 24 and 25.

28

Place and close an open jump ring through the 7th vertical closed jump ring and the 2 closed jump rings added in steps 25 and 26.

29

Place and close an open jump ring through a new closed jump ring, the 8th vertical closed jump ring, and the closed jump ring that was added in step 24.

30

Place and close an open jump ring through a new closed jump ring, the 9th vertical closed jump ring ,and the closed jump ring that was added in step 25.

31

Place and close an open jump ring through a new closed jump ring, the 10th vertical closed jump ring and the closed jump ring added in step 26.

32

Place and close an open jump ring through the 11th vertical closed jump ring and the 2 closed jump rings added in steps 29 and 30.

33

Place and close an open jump ring through the 12th vertical closed jump ring and the 2 closed jump rings added in steps 30 and 31.

Note: The top of the small square has returned to its original arrangement of links, consisting of 9 horizontal jump rings and 12 vertical jump rings.

34 Repeat steps 10 through 33 to complete the square's transformation into a fully three-dimensional cube.

35 To create a 2nd cube, repeat steps 2 through 34.

To create the short chain for the 1st cube:

36

Place and close an open large jump ring (B) through the closed small jump ring added to the cube in step 23. Repeat with a 2nd open jump ring.

37

Place and close an open small jump ring (A) through 2 closed large jump rings (B) and the 2 large jump rings (B) added in the previous step.

38 | Repeat step 37 a total of 19 times, adding a total of 20 large jump ring (B) pairs to the short chain.

39 | Repeat steps 36 through 38 to create a 2nd short chain.
　　　Set the 1st cube aside.

To create the long chains for the 2nd cube:

40 | Repeat steps 36 and 37, except repeat step 38 a total of 26 times, instead of 19, adding a total of 27 large jump ring (B) pairs to the long chain.
　　　Set the 2nd cube aside.

41 | Following the instructions on page 15, make 2 head pin and bead combinations with the focus beads.

42 |

Place and close an open large jump ring (B) through the loop of a headpin and bead combination and the 3 closed small jump rings (A) from the opposite edge of the cube as the closed small jump ring (A) added in step 23. Repeat for the 2nd cube.

43 |

Place the 1st cube with short chains above the 2nd cube with long chains. Bring all 4 chains around so that the final pairs of closed large jump rings (B) are aligned with the slide clasp.

44 | Place and close a small jump ring (A) through the final pair of closed large jump rings (B) from the left-hand long chain and the top left loop of the slide clasp.

45 | Place and close a small jump ring (A) through the final pair of closed large jump rings (B) from the right-hand long chain and the top right loop of the slide clasp.

46 | Place and close a small jump ring (A) through the final pair of closed large jump rings (B) from the left-hand short chain and the bottom left loop of the slide clasp.

47 |

Place and close a small jump ring (A) through the final pair of closed large jump rings (B) from the right-hand short chain and the bottom right loop of the slide clasp.
　　　Remove any ring markers.

Rain
Earrings

Designed by **Ruslana Zitserman**

These sophisticated and complex-looking earrings are constructed with asymmetrical, flat chain mail. The flat mail is joined to create a dimensional form adorned with dangling pearls.

Basic Pattern: European 4-1 Inlay

ADVANCED

YOU WILL NEED

- 38 small sterling silver jump rings, 22 gauge (0.6426 mm), 2.8 mm i.d.
- 150 large sterling silver jump rings, 20 gauge (0.8128 mm), 3 mm i.d.
- 112 copper jump rings, 20 gauge (0.8128 mm), 3 mm i.d.
- #12 bead stringing wire
- 25 sterling silver crimp beads
- 6 large freshwater pearls
- 8 small freshwater pearls
- 50 seamless sterling silver beads, 2mm
- 1 pair ear wires
- Chain-nose pliers
- Flush cutting wire snips

1 | Open 28 small sterling silver jump rings and close 10 small sterling silver jump rings. Close 10 large sterling silver jump rings.

2 |

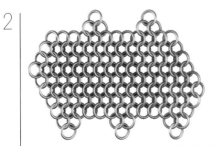

Review the instructions for 4-1 chain mail on page 18. Create a piece of European 4-1 chain mail from 70 large sterling silver jump rings and 56 copper jump rings using the chart as a guide.

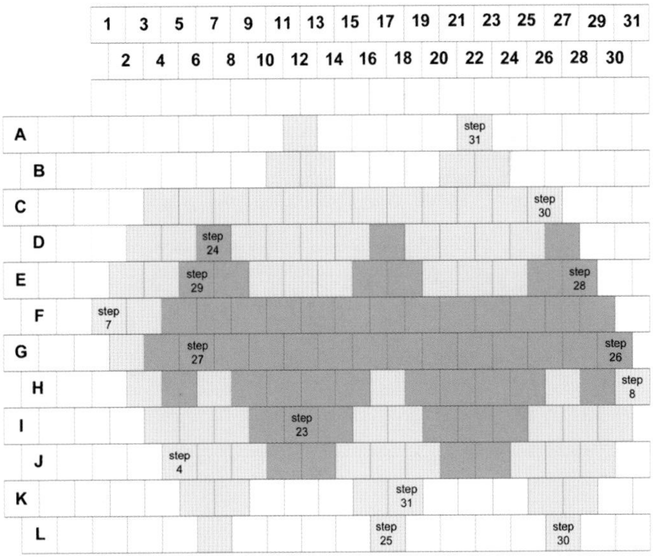

Chart (columns 1–31, rows A–L):

Row	Step locations (column)
1 3 5 7 9 11 13 15 17 19 21 23 25 27 29 31	
2 4 6 8 10 12 14 16 18 20 22 24 26 28 30	
A	step 31 (col 21)
B	
C	step 30 (col 24)
D	step 24 (col 9)
E	step 29 (col 9), step 28 (col 26)
F	step 7 (col 1)
G	step 27 (col 6), step 26 (col 28)
H	step 8 (col 28)
I	step 23 (col 12)
J	step 4 (col 5)
K	step 31 (col 16)
L	step 25 (col 15), step 30 (col 24)

Note: The chart uses letters to designate row location and numbers to designate column location. Gray squares represent large silver jump rings and orange squares represent copper jump rings.

3 | Place and close an open small jump ring through 2 closed small jump rings.

4 |

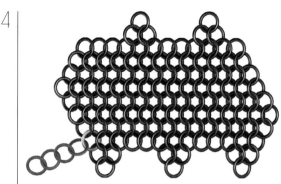

Place and close an open small jump ring through 1 of the closed small jump rings from step 3 and the large jump ring J5 on the chain mail piece.

5 | Place and close an open small jump ring through 3 new closed small jump rings.

6 | Place and close an open small jump ring through 1 of the closed small jump rings from step 5.

7 |

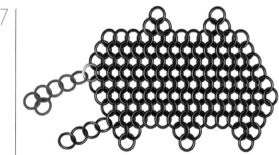

Place and close an open small jump ring through the small jump ring added in step 6 and the large jump ring F1 on the chain mail piece.

8 |

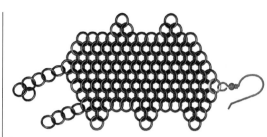

Reopen jump ring H31, place the loop of an ear wire on jump ring H31 and reclosed this ring. Set the chain mail piece aside.

9 | Cut twelve 6-inch lengths of beading wire.

10 | Create 6 single-drop strands of various lengths by threading a crimp bead on a length of beading wire. Crimp the bead in place at one end of the wire. Add a pearl, and a few seamless beads, and finish with a crimp bead. Fold the wire back over a large jump ring and thread it back through the crimp bead. Adjust the wire to the desired length, then crimp the bead and trim the wire.

11 | Create 4 double-drop strands by threading a crimp bead on the end of a wire. Crimp it in place. Thread a pearl, a bead, and crimp bead on the wire. Thread the wire through a large jump ring. Bring the wire back through the crimp bead and the end of the wire even with the opposite end. Crimp the bead. Add seamless beads, a pearl, and a crimp bead to the end of the wire. Place a crimp bead on the end of the wire and crimp in place.

12 | Place and close an open small jump ring through jump ring I12 on the chain mail piece and the large closed jump ring of the 1st double bead drop.

13 | Place and close an open small jump ring through jump ring D7 on the chain mail piece and the large closed jump ring of the 2nd double bead drop.

14 | Place and close an open small jump ring through jump ring L17 on the chain mail piece and the large closed jump ring of the 7.5 cm bead drop.

15 | Place and close an open small jump ring through jump ring G30 on the chain mail piece and the large closed jump ring of the 8.5 cm bead drop.

16 | Place an open small jump ring through jump ring G6 on the chain mail piece, then place the bead wire from the 8.5 cm bead drop through the small open jump ring and close.

17 | Place and close an open small jump ring through jump ring E28 on the chain mail piece and the large closed jump ring of the 9.5 cm bead drop.

18 | Place an open small jump ring through jump ring E6 on the chain mail piece, then place the bead wire from the 9.5 cm bead drop through the small open jump ring and close.

19 | Bringing the 2 sides of the chain mail piece together, place and close an open small jump ring through jump rings L27 and C26.

20 | Bringing the 2 sides of the chain mail piece together, place and close an open small jump ring through jump rings A22 and K18.

21 | Repeat steps 2 through 20 to create the 2nd earring, except flip the chain mail piece created in step 2 and reverse the placement of the drop beads to create a mirror image.

Japanese
Hexagonal
Mail Collar

eth Tokoly

Dense and complex, this variation on Japanese mail construction is well worth the effort and time it takes to assemble.

YOU WILL NEED

1228 sterling silver jump rings, 20 gauge (0.8128 mm), 3.95 mm i.d.

Toggle clasp

Chain-nose pliers

1 | Close 27 jump rings and open 126 jump rings.

2 |

Place and close an open jump ring through 2 closed jump rings. Repeat, placing and closing a 2nd open jump ring through the same 2 closed jump rings.

3 |
Place and close an open jump ring through a new closed jump ring and 1 closed jump ring from the previous step. Repeat, placing and closing a 2nd open jump ring through the same closed jump rings

4 |

Repeat step 3 to create a short chain that has a total of 4 horizontal jump rings.

5 | Repeat steps 2 through 4 five times to create a total of 6 short chains that have a 4 horizontal jump rings each.

6 | Repeat steps 2 through 3 once to create a short chain that has 3 horizontal jump rings.

7 |

Place 2 of the 4-horizontal-jump-ring chains side by side, with the lower chain offset to the right as shown.

8 |

Place and close an open jump ring through the 1st horizontal jump ring of the top chain and the 1st horizontal jump ring of the bottom chain. Repeat, placing and closing a 2nd open jump ring through the same closed jump rings.

9 |

Place and close an open jump ring through the 1st horizontal jump ring of the bottom chain and the 2nd horizontal jump ring of the top chain. Repeat, placing and closing a 2nd open jump ring through the same closed jump rings.

10

Continue adding pairs of rings until the chains are connected.

11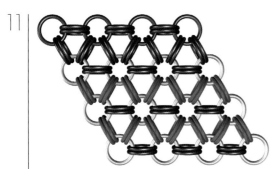

Repeat steps 8 through 10 twice, placing a new 4-horizontal-jump-ring chain below the connected chains, offset to the right, before you start, until you have a section of mail in the shape of a parallelogram.

12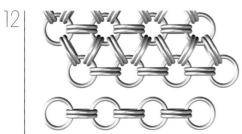

Place 1 of the 4-horizontal-ring chains below the parallelogram, offset to the left as shown.

13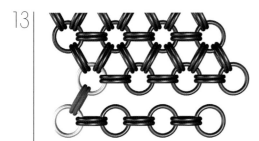

Place and close an open jump ring through the 1st horizontal jump ring of the top parallelogram and the 1st horizontal jump ring of the bottom chain. Repeat, placing and closing a 2nd open jump ring through the same closed jump rings.

14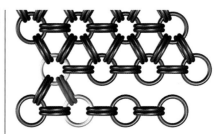

Place and close an open jump ring through the 1st horizontal jump ring of the top parallelogram and the 2nd horizontal jump ring of the bottom chain. Repeat, placing and closing a 2nd open jump ring through the same closed jump rings.

15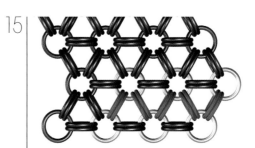

Continue adding pairs of rings until both chains are connected.

16 Repeat steps 12 through 15.

17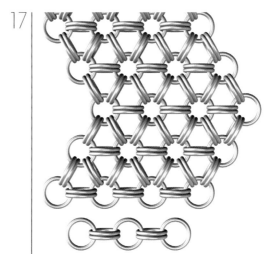

Place the 3-horizontal-ring chain below the emerging chevron shape, as shown.

18

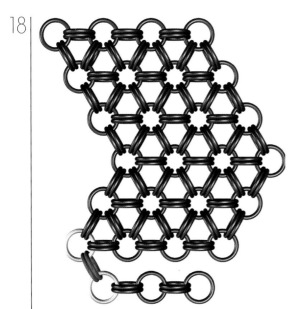

Place and close an open jump ring through the 1st horizontal jump ring of the top chevron and the 1st horizontal jump ring of the bottom chain. Repeat, placing and closing a 2nd open jump ring through the same closed jump rings.

19

Place and close an open jump ring through the 1st horizontal jump ring of the bottom chain and the 2nd horizontal jump ring of the top chevron. Repeat, placing and closing a 2nd open jump ring through the same closed jump rings.

20

Continue adding pairs of rings until the bottom chain is completely connected.

21 | Repeat steps 1 through 20 a total of 8 more times to create 8 chevron shapes.

Note: The shapes created are not perfect chevrons.

22

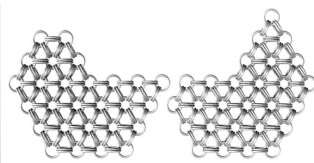

Place 2 chevrons side by side so that the top right horizontal ring of the left chevron completes the top left corner of the right chevron, as shown.

23

Place and close an open jump ring through the top right horizontal ring of the left chevron and the next horizontal ring of the right chevron, as shown. Repeat, placing and closing a 2nd open jump ring through the same closed jump rings.

24

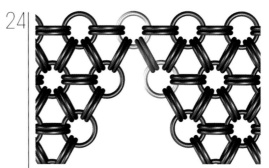

Place and close an open jump ring through the top right horizontal ring of the left chevron and the remaining horizontal ring of the right chevron, as shown. Repeat, placing and closing a 2nd open jump ring through the same closed jump rings.

25 | Repeat steps 22 through 24 for the remaining 6 chevrons to complete a continuous choker with a total of 8 chevrons.

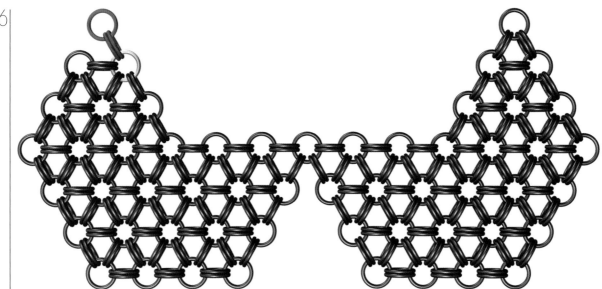

Place and close an open jump ring through a
new closed jump ring and the top left closed
jump ring of the leftmost chevron. Repeat,
placing and closing a second open jump ring
through the same closed jump rings.

27|

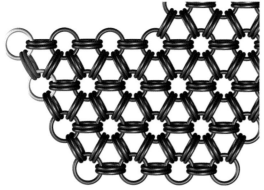

Place and close an open jump ring through the
new closed jump ring added in step 25 and
the leftmost top closed jump ring of the leftmost
chevron. Repeat, placing and closing a second
open jump ring through the same closed
jump rings.

28| Open 4 jump rings. Place and close an open
jump ring through the top right horizontal ring of
the choker and one half of the toggle clasp.
Repeat, placing and closing a 2nd open jump
ring through the same jump ring and the same
half of the toggle clasp.

29| Place and close an open jump ring through
the top left horizontal ring of the choker and the
other half of the toggle clasp. Repeat, placing
and closing a 2nd open jump ring through
the same jump ring and same half of the
toggle clasp.

Tasseled Snake Lariat

Designed by **Cheryl Fulcher**

This slinky chain is ingeniously constructed flat, then folded and joined with single rings up the open seam to make a tube. Create a unique tassel with your favorite gemstone beads or pearls.

YOU WILL NEED

742 large sterling silver jump rings, 16 gauge (1.291 mm), 4.5 mm i.d. (A)

162 small sterling silver jump rings, 18 gauge (1.024 mm), 2.4 mm i.d. (B)

1 oversized sterling silver jump ring, 12 gauge (2.052 mm), 12.7 mm i.d. (C)*

9 beads

9 headpins

Flat-nose pliers

Round-nose pliers

Flush cutting wire snips

* For strength, purchase a soldered jump ring or have the ring soldered.

1 Close 369 large jump rings (A) and open 373 large jump rings (A). Close 81 small jump rings (B) and open 90 small jump rings (B).

2 Create a length of European 4-1 chain mail with large jump rings (A) using the chainlet method described on page 18. The length should be 123 edge rings long and 5 rows wide.

3

Place and close an open large jump ring through the top and middle end jump rings at 1 end of the chain, as shown.

4

Place and close an open large jump ring through the middle and bottom end jump rings from the end of the chain.

5

Place and close an open large jump ring through the 2 large jump rings added in steps 3 and 4 and the oversized jump ring. Repeat, placing and closing another open large jump ring through the same 2 large jump rings added in steps 3 and 4 and the same oversized jump ring.

6

Fold the chain in half lengthwise.

7 | Place and close an open large jump ring through the 1st and 2nd large jump rings on the left side of the chain and the 1st and 2nd jump rings on the right side of the chain.

8 | Place and close an open large jump ring through the 2nd and 3rd large jump rings on the left side of the chain and the 2nd and 3rd large jump rings on the right side of the chain.

9 | Repeat step 8 down the length of the chain to attach the sides and create a round snake chain.

10 | Place and close an open large jump ring vertically through the large jump ring added in step 7.

11 | Place and close an open large jump ring through the large jump ring added in step 10 and the oversized jump ring. Repeat, placing and closing an open large jump ring through the same large jump ring added in step 10 and the same oversized jump ring.

12 | Slip the beads onto the head pins and create wrapped bead loops (see page 15).

13 | Place and close an open small jump ring (B) through each head pin's wrapped loop.

14 | Place and close an open small jump ring (B) through a new closed small jump ring and a closed small jump ring attached to a head pin and bead combination.

15 | Place and close an open small jump ring (B) through a new closed small jump ring and the last closed small jump ring from the previous step.

Add 6 more small rings to create a chain 17 rings in length.

16 | Repeat steps 13 through 15 with the remaining wrapped wire loops.

17 | Place and close an open small jump ring through the small jump ring at the end of one of the chains and a large jump ring that tilts inward at the end of the round snake chain. Repeat twice, attaching 2 more chains to the same large jump ring.

Add 3 chains to each of the 2 remaining large rings that tilt inward.

KIRSTYN MCDERMOTT

Katherine, 2004

Adjustable, 12½ to 15¾ inches (32 to 40 cm)
Stainless steel, Czech crystal beads; Bzyantine weave
Photo © artist

COLLEEN BARAN

Punk Princess, 2003

13¼ x 18¼ x ³/₁₆ inches (33.5 x 46.5 x 0.5 cm)
Sterling silver; hand fabricated
Photo © artist

KIRSTYN MCDERMOTT

Clio, 2004

Inner length, 18 inches (46 cm)
Stainless steel, amethyst beads, Bali silver spacer beads,
sterling silver wire; box weave
Photo © artist

DONOVAN WIDMER

Umbrella, 2003

52 x 52 x 60 inches (cm)
Copper, stainless steel, aluminum,
brass; Hana Gusari 6-2 pattern
Photo © Dennis French

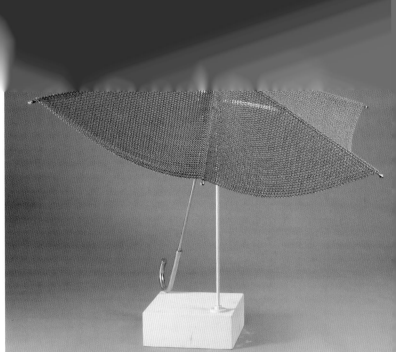

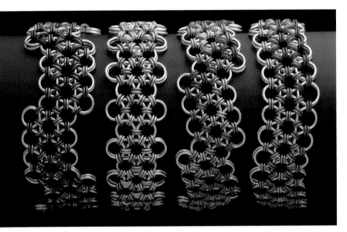

SPIDER

Four Bracelets: Earth, Air, Fire, Water, 2005

Each, ¾ x 7½ inches (1.9 x 19 cm)
Anodized niobium, gold-fill, sterling silver;
Japanese 12-2
Photo © artist

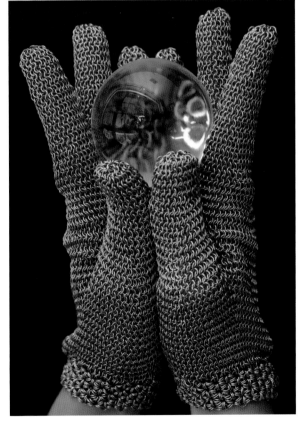

CHRISTINE DHEIN

Soft Spike Arm Cuff, 1998

7½ x 2½ x ½ inches (19 x 6.4 x 1.3 cm)
Sterling silver, rubber; hand fabricated, chain
mail technique, roller printed, riveted
Photo © Don Felton

SPIDER

Gloves, 1996–2001

Medium glove size
Stainless steel; European 4-1, Japanese 12-2, soldered
Photo © Tanya Anguita

MYRA MIMLITSCH-GRAY

Gold Ball Ring, 1999

1 x ¾ x ¾ inches (2.5 x 1.9 x 1.9 cm)
18-karat gold; fabricated, formed
Photo © Robert Storm

LISA FORTIN/STEEL COUTURE

Hematite Collar, 2002

4 inches (10.2 cm) wide; neck circumference, 16 inches (40.6 cm)
Nickel-plated rings; saw cut, 8-1 European, 4-1
Photo © Justin Guarino

MYRA MIMLITSCH-GRAY

Round Chain Mail Cuff, 1999

3 x 3 x 1 inches (7.6 x 7.6 x 2.5 cm)
Silver, 14-karat white gold; fabricated, forged
Photo © Robert Storm

MYRA MIMLITSCH-GRAY

Fish Server, 2000

12 x 3½ x 2 inches (30.5 x 8.9 x 5.1 cm)
Silver; cast, hot forged, fabricated
Photo © artist
Collection of Seymour Rabinovitch

MYRA MIMLITSCH-GRAY

Large Chain Mail Cuff, 1999

3 x 3 x 1½ inches (7.6 x 7.6 x 3.8 cm)
Silver; fabricated, forged
Photo © Robert Storm

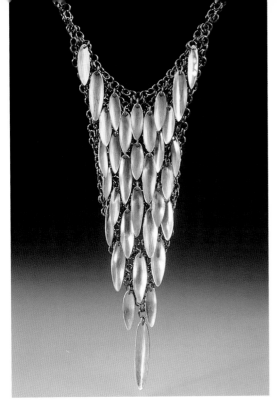

DINA VARANO

Cascade, 2005

16 x 5 x 7¼ inches (40.6 x 12.7 x 18.4 cm)
14-karat gold, sterling silver; fabricated, oxidized
Photo © Mark Johnson

ELAINE UNZICKER

Sterling Cross Necklace, 2000

16 inches (40.6 cm) in diameter
Sterling silver, cross pearl; chain mail technique
Photo © Allen Bryan

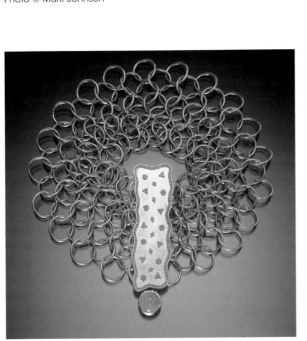

JILL HURANT

Chainmail Bracelet, 2002

7 x 1½ inches (17.8 x 3.8 cm)
20-karat gold, 22-karat gold, aquamarine;
hand fabricated, granulation
Photo © Ralph Gabriner

ANDREW TELESCA

Slave Choker, 2005

1¼ x 1 x ⅜ inches (3.2 x 2.5 x 1 cm)
Brass, stainless steel; European 4-1, Oriental simple chains
Photo © artist

HISANO TAKEI

Scarf and Brooch Set #2, 2001

Scarf, 2 x 34½ inches (5.1 x 87.6 cm);
brooch, 4 x ¾ inches (10.2 x 1.9 cm)
Sterling silver, freshwater pearls; fabricated,
handmade jump rings, chain mail technique
Photo © Barry Blau

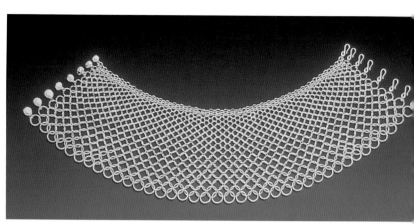

HISANO TAKEI

Choker, 2001

3½ x 14 x ½ inches (8.9 x 35.6 x 1.3 cm)
Sterling silver, moonstones; fabricated, bezel set,
handmade jump rings, chain mail technique
Photo © Barry Blau

ELAINE UNZICKER

2-Inch-Wide Tiny Pod Bracelet, 2003

2 x 7 inches (5.1 x 17.8 cm)
Stainless steel, brass, gold, sterling silver; cast, plated,
chain mail technique
Photo © Allen Bryan

ELIZABETH ANN TOKOLY

Anamorskeltesseract, 1998

4 x 8 x 4 inches (10.2 x 20.4 x 10.2 cm)
Nickel silver; queen's chains
Photo © artist and Melinda Amann

CHRISTINE DHEIN

White Nile Neckpiece #2, 2000

10 x 6 x ¼ inches (25.4 x 15.2 x 0.6 cm)
24-karat gold, 14-karat gold, sterling silver, rubber,
diamonds; hand fabricated, flat chain mail technique,
riveted, tube set
Photo © Don Felton

ELAINE UNZICKER

Catalpa Collar, 1994

16 inches (40.6 cm) in diameter
Stainless steel, cast brass, gold; cast, plated,
chain mail technique
Photo © Allen Bryan

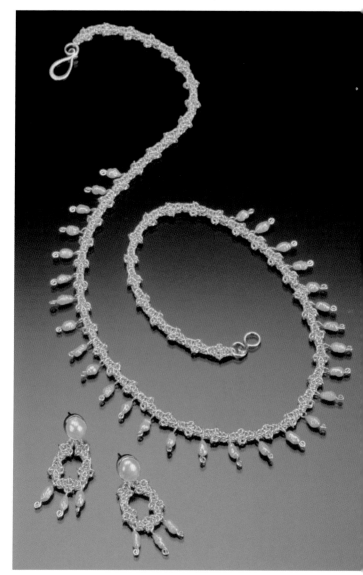

JULIA ANN LOWTHER

Fine Cross Chain Necklace and Earrings

Necklace, 19 inches (48.3 cm) long;
earrings, 1½ x ½ inches (3.8 x 1.3 cm)
Sterling silver, fine silver, freshwater pearls; linked
handmade jump rings
Photo © Doug Yaple

Designer Biographies

2-Roses Studio, located in Southern California, is a lifelong artistic exploration and collaboration between metalsmith Corliss Rose and lapidary John Lemieux Rose. Each is a master craftsperson with a distinctive style and unique artistic vision. Visit their website at www.2rosesstudios.com.

Rachel Dow is a jewelry artist specializing in fabricated silver, metal clay, and found object jewelry. She received a BA in Photography and an MA in art education from California State University of Northridge. When she's not banging on metal, she's running around with her three-year-old son and working with fiber. Visit her website at www.rmddesigns.com.

John Fetvedt translates his interest in art, mathematics, and 3-D jigsaw puzzles into creating fine chain mail jewelry that feels "soft and sensuous" on the human body. He teaches and exhibits his work in Raleigh, North Carolina. Visit his website at www.jef.com.

Growing up in West Vancouver, Canada, **Cheryl Fulcher** developed a natural attraction to the flow and balance of nature. With the background of her father's ability to improvise and her mother's eye for precision, Cheryl was destined for creativity. All it took was a basic jewelry course for her to become a perpetual student. Recently, Cheryl has stepped away from working with traditional metals and is experimenting with stainless steel and neoprene rubber.

Elizabeth Hake's work has appeared in *Metalsmith*, *Lapidary Journal*, *Art Jewelry Now* by Dona Meilach, and *Found Object Jewelry* (Lark, 2005). In 2002–2003 she was an artist-in-residence at Arrowmont School of Arts and Crafts in Gatlinburg, Tennessee. She has taught jewelry classes at Arrowmont and at John C. Campbell Folk School in Brasstown, North Carolina. She lives in Asheville, North Carolina.

Anne M. Kelly has called the west coast of Canada home since 1967. In the mid-1990s a car accident changed her life. While adapting to a set of new physical limitations, she became fascinated with the art of weaving chain mail. She began working with metal and gemstones to create wearable art. Anne has a degree in creative writing from the University of Victoria, where she was awarded the Victoria Medal for achievement in Fine Arts. Her jewelry is sold in art galleries and by custom order.

Ingrid I. van der Meer-Groen has been making things since she was a child in the Netherlands. In 2002 she began taking jewelry, silversmithing, and enameling classes—at her sister's suggestion—at the Glassell School of Arts in Houston, Texas. She now runs her own jewelry business, Double Eye Design.

While backpacking through Europe, **Rebecca Mojica** saw several people wearing belts made of chain mail. She couldn't purchase one, so she learned to make one herself. Since then she has added more than just a belt to her repertoire: sculptures, juggling cubes, jewelry, and more, all made of chain mail. You can view more of her work at www.bluebuddhaboutique.com.

Stephanie Morton began her jewelry career 15 years ago when she couldn't find a ring that she wanted. She decided to make it herself. She took a night course in wax carving and successfully made the ring. That first course was so enjoyable that she continued taking courses and soon found herself addicted to the art of making jewelry. She's continually inspired and amazed by the never-ending learning process and happily continues to explore each facet.

Jerry Penner is a self-taught chain mail artist living in New Hamburg, Ontario, Canada. He began making chain mail after seeing Tina Turner's dress in the film *Mad Max Beyond Thunderdome*. Since then, he's been making way-out fashion and intricate jewelry with chain mail. Visit his website at www.chainmailguy.com.

Emily Shore has been making jewelry out of wire since she was 10. She's tried many techniques, from stringing simple beads to crochet and, most recently, chain mail. She sells her chain mail jewelry at the New Jersey Renaissance Kingdom, local festivals and creates custom pieces for clients. She lives in Metuchen, New Jersey.

Acknowledgments

Spider is a chain mail artist currently living in the San Francisco Bay area. She has a degree in mechanical engineering from MIT. After several years of working with computers, she discovered that her passion lay not in technology, but in art. Today she spends her time discovering new and beautiful ways to weave metal. Visit her website at www.spiderchain.com.

Andrew Telesca began crafting chain mail in 2001 and started his own business, Maile of the Dreamseeker, in the Spring of 2002 as a way to finance his art. He lives in Walla Walla, Washington. Visit his website at www.maileofthedreamseeker.com

Elizabeth Tokoly has taught jewelry and metalwork for the past six years at the 92nd Street Y in New York, New York. She lives in Jersey City, New Jersey, where she operates Studio No. 159 The Fine Art of Design. Her studio offerrs people handmade objects and teaches them the importance of texture, color, form, and spirit through interior design, decorative painting, and freelance artwork.

Dylon Whyte has been studying and making original chain mail creations and patterns since 1986—he was 12. Dylon's self-published *The Art of Chainmail: Volume I, European Patterns*, took more than four years to research, write, and illustrate. He operates his own computer repair and Web design business in addition to pursuing lapidary work and designing chain mail. He's a lifelong resident of Manitoulin Island, Canada. Visit his website at www.artofchainmail.com.

Ruslana Zitserman and her family emigrated to the United States in 1987 from the Ukraine. She has an MA in computer science with a minor in East Asian Religions. Her passion for jewelry became a full-time occupation in 1999, when her company and label Ateh Modus Vivendi were founded. Ruslana is a member of Society of North American Goldsmiths (SNAG), PMC Guild, and Jewelry Design Professionals' Network (JDPN). She lives in Rego Park, New York.

Many thanks to all of the project designers for their creativity, enthusiasm, and patience while we put together *Chain Mail Jewelry*.

Thanks to Jon Daniels at www.theringlord.com for providing us with samples of a wide variety of rings to photograph.

Thank you, Dylon, for expertly decoding everyone's instructions. Let's go have a drink now.

Key to Wire Gauges

The projects in this book were made using wire manufactured in the United States, whose standards for wire diameters differ from those in the British system. AWG is the acronym for American, or Brown & Sharpe, wire gauge sizes and their equivalent rounded metric measurements. SWG is the acronym for the British Standard, or Imperial, system in the UK. Refer to the chart below if you use SWG wire. Only part of the full range of wire gauges that are available from jewelry suppliers is included here.

AWG in.	AWG mm	Gauge	SWG in.	SWG mm
0.204	5.18	4	0.232	5.89
0.182	4.62	5	0.212	5.38
0.162	4.12	6	0.192	4.88
0.144	3.66	7	0.176	4.47
0.129	3.28	8	0.160	4.06
0.114	2.90	9	0.144	3.66
0.102	2.59	10	0.128	3.25
0.091	2.31	11	0.116	2.95
0.081	2.06	12	0.104	2.64
0.072	1.83	13	0.092	2.34
0.064	1.63	14	0.080	2.03
0.057	1.45	15	0.072	1.83
0.051	1.30	16	0.064	1.63
0.045	1.14	17	0.056	1.42
0.040	1.02	18	0.048	1.22
0.036	0.914	19	0.040	1.02
0.032	0.813	20	0.036	0.914
0.029	0.737	21	0.032	0.813
0.025	0.635	22	0.028	0.711
0.023	0.584	23	0.024	0.610
0.020	0.508	24	0.022	0.559
0.018	0.457	25	0.020	0.508
0.016	0.406	26	0.018	0.457

Index